DORLING KINDERSLEY 📖 EYEWITNESS BOOKS

AZTEC, INCA
& MAYA

Peruvian mummy cloth

Aztec sacrificial knife

Mesoamerican farming tools

Ceremonial urn showing Chaac, Maya god of rain

Aztec ceramic flute

Marigolds, given as offerings to goddesses by the Aztecs

Moche vessel showing fisherman in boat

Peruvian silver portrait beaker

Olmec jade mask

DK EYEWITNESS BOOKS

Mortar and pestle
with chilli

AZTEC, INCA
& MAYA

Written by
ELIZABETH BAQUEDANO

Photographed by
MICHEL ZABÉ

Aztec army commander

Toltec coyote
warrior inlaid with
mother-of-pearl

Aztec
skull mask

Inca necklace made with
turquoise, shell, and gold beads

Dorling Kindersley

Warrior wearing feather headdress

Zapotec jade
necklace

Chancay
textile doll

Dorling Kindersley

LONDON, NEW YORK, AUCKLAND, DELHI, JOHANNESBURG,
MUNICH, PARIS and SYDNEY

For a full catalog, visit

DK www.dk.com

Project editor Christine Webb
Art editor Andrew Nash
Managing editor Helen Parker
Managing art editor Julia Harris
Production Catherine Semark
Picture research Cynthia Hole
Researcher Céline Carez
Additional photography Andy Crawford and Dave Rudkin

This Eyewitness ® Book has been conceived by
Dorling Kindersley Limited and Editions Gallimard

© 1993 Dorling Kindersley Limited
This edition © 2000 Dorling Kindersley Limited
First American edition, 1993

Published in the United States by
Dorling Kindersley Publishing, Inc.
95 Madison Avenue
New York, NY 10016
2 4 6 8 10 9 7 5 3

Dorling Kindersley books are available at special discounts for bulk purchases
for sales promotions or premiums. Special editions, including personalized
covers, excerpts of existing guides, and corporate imprints can be created in
large quantities for specific needs. For more information, contact Special
Markets Dept., Dorling Kindersley Publishing, Inc., 95 Madison Ave.,
New York, NY 10016; Fax: (800) 600-9098

Library of Congress Cataloging-in-Publication Data
Baquedano, Elizabeth.
Aztec, Inca & Maya / written by Elizabeth Baquedano.
p. cm. — (Eyewitness Books)
Includes index.
Summary: Chronicles the history, beliefs, and everyday lives of the
ancient Aztec, Inca, and Maya peoples.
1. Aztecs—Juvenile literature. 2. Mayas—Juvenile literature.
3. Incas—Juvenile literature. [1. Aztecs. 2. Mayas. 3. Incas. 4. Indians
of Mexico. 5. Indians of Central America. 6. Indians of South America.]
I. Title. II. Title: Aztec, Inca and Maya.
F1219.73B35 2000
972'.018—dc20
ISBN 0-7894-6116-1 (pb)
ISBN 0-7894-6115-3 (hb)

Color reproduction by Colourscan, Singapore
Printed in China by Toppan Printing Co. (Shenzhen) Ltd.

Toltec
warrior

Peruvian
feather fan

Mixtec head

Ancient Peruvian feather headdress

Contents

Chacmool from
the Great Temple
of the Aztecs

Aztecs, Mayas, and Incas

I**N THE 16TH CENTURY**, Spanish explorers in the Americas encountered two great civilizations – one in Mesoamerica (the territory controlled by the Aztecs and the Mayas at the time of the conquest) and the other in South America (the territory in the central Andean region under Inca rule). The people of these regions were a mosaic of tribes and nations, whose great achievements included masterpieces of art, spectacular cities, and a unique approach to life. The strong foundations of economic, political, and social organization typical of each of these empires had already been laid by earlier American cultures.

THE MAYA PEOPLE
The Maya kingdom emerged around 1000 B.C., and lasted until A.D. 1697. All Mayas shared a common culture and religion, but they did not have a sole capital city or ruler. Each city governed itself and had its own noble ruler. Mayan figurines like this one, from the island of Jaina, have been a great source of information on the life and customs of the Maya people.

Ornate necklace

Large, heavy earplugs

Mayan clay figurine of powerful man

The Mayas were short and robust. They had slanting dark eyes and black hair

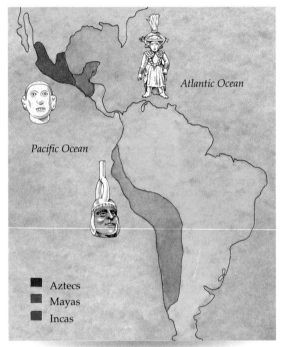

Atlantic Ocean

Pacific Ocean

■ Aztecs
■ Mayas
■ Incas

MIDDLE AND SOUTH AMERICA
The Aztec empire, with its capital at Tenochtitlán, stretched between the Pacific and the Atlantic coasts of Mesoamerica, while the Maya kingdom occupied the eastern part of Mesoamerica. The Inca empire stretched 4,000 miles (2,500 km) along the west coast of South America .

LEARNED MAYAS
The Mayas were distinguished in arithmetic and astronomy, as well as having their own hieroglyphic writing (pp. 40–41). The four Mayan codices that exist today, however, tell us little of their history; they focus on subjects such as rituals, astronomy, and calendars.

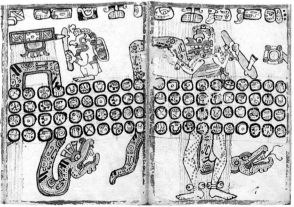

Mayan codex

THE FOUNDING OF TENOCHTITLAN

According to Aztec mythology, Huitzilopochtli, their tribal god, promised to show his people the place where they were to settle and build their great capital, Tenochtitlán. He told them to look for an eagle perched upon a cactus with a serpent in its beak. This would be a sign that they had found their promised land. The first page of the Codex Mendoza (a book telling the history of the Aztecs) illustrates the foundation of Tenochtitlán in either 1325 or 1345. Mexico City is built on the same site.

INCA GOLD

The Incas excelled at working metals such as silver, copper, and gold (pp. 50–51). Female figures like this one have been found with Inca offerings to the gods.

Wooden cup, or *kero*, with decoration of Inca man holding spear and shield

THE AZTECS

The Aztecs were a wandering tribe before they settled in the Valley of Mexico on swampy land in Lake Texcoco and founded Tenochtitlán. It grew in size and importance until it became the capital of the mighty Aztec empire. The Aztecs conquered many people, demanding tribute from them (pp. 26–27). The Aztecs were short and stocky, with brown skin and broad faces.

Aztecs had thick black hair

THE ANDEAN PEOPLE

The Inca empire developed the most important state in the Andean highlands in 1438, when they conquered the area around the city Cuzco and made it their capital. The Incas conquered provinces and incorporated them into their empire. Due to their efficient administration system, they kept control over all their empire. The people of the Andean area were typically small, with straight black hair and brown skin.

Almond-shaped eyes

High cheekbones

Even, white teeth

Aquiline nose

Stone sculpture of Aztec head

Moche clay portrait vessel

People of Mesoamerica

WARRING AZTECS
At its height, the Aztec empire was strong and prosperous. Conquered areas were controlled by the powerful Aztec army. This illustration shows an army commander.

MESOAMERICA is one of two areas in the Americas (the other being the central Andes) that had urban civilizations, or "high cultures," at the time of the Spanish conquest in 1519. The fact that Mesoamericans built spectacular pyramids and temples (pp. 30–31), had large markets (pp. 26–27), the ball-game (pp. 58–59), a sacred calendar, hieroglyphic writing (pp. 40–41), and a group of gods (pp. 32–33); and practiced human sacrifice (pp. 36–37) sets Mesoamerica apart from its neighbors. Mesoamerican cultural history is divided into three main periods: the Preclassic, the Classic, and the Postclassic, stretching from about 2000 B.C. until the Spanish conquest (pp. 62–63). During these periods Mesoamerica saw the rise and fall of many civilizations. The Olmecs were the dominant culture in the Preclassic period. The Classic period saw the rise of the mighty Teotihuacán culture and the Mayas. The Postclassic period was one of militarism, and warring empires, such as the Toltecs and Aztecs.

MAYAN RITUAL
Religion was the center of every Mayan person's life. One of the major achievements of the Mayas was the construction of superb temples and other buildings to honor their gods. These were decorated with carvings such as this lintel showing a woman drawing blood from her tongue. Self-sacrifice was common throughout Mesoamerica.

MAP OF MESOAMERICA
Mesoamerica is both a geographical and a cultural region. At the time of the Spanish conquest it included what is now central and southern Mexico and the peninsula of Yucatán, Guatemala, Belize, El Salvador, the westernmost part of Honduras, and a small part of Nicaragua and northern Costa Rica.

Gulf of Mexico

Yucatán Peninsula

Chichén Itzá •

Toltecs   • *Tula*
   •*Teotihuacán*
Tenochtitlán •
Lake Texcoco   • *Veracruz*   **Mayans**

Olmecs   *Tikal* •
Mixtecs   *Palenque* •

Monte Alban •   **Zapotecs**

Pacific Ocean

THE TOLTECS
The Toltec civilization, with its capital at Tula, flourished about A.D. 900–1187. The Toltecs were masters of architecture and the arts. They were also a great warring society, as can be seen in their many sculptures of warriors. This warrior (left) has raised arms for holding an altar or shrine. The Toltecs had a great influence in Mayan territory during the Postclassic period, and there are similarities in some of their sculpture and architecture.

THE MIXTECS
The history of the Mixtec civilization can be traced back in codices to the 7th century A.D.; the Miztecs existed until the Spanish conquest. They produced superb pottery, and were very concerned with history, and writing about their origins in codices (pp. 40–41), many of which still survive.

The Mixtecs are famous for their decorated pottery

This type of decoration is similar to the images in Mixtec codices

TEOTIHUACAN

The Teotihuacán culture flourished between A.D. 1 and 750. The city Teotihuacán is the most impressive city to be seen in the Americas.

The Teotihuacán culture was the most influential culture in Mesoamerica. We know little about the physical appearance of the people, but the masks found at Teotihuacán give us a good idea of what they looked like.

Hole in earlobe for earring

Masks may have been portraits of the dead

Greenstone mask from Teotihuacán

Head made of basalt is 5 ft (1.5 m) tall and weighs more than 20 tons

COLOSSAL HEAD

Several heads such as this one have been found in the Olmec heartland in the Gulf Coast region. They may be the heads of ball-game players, or "portraits" of rulers or chiefs.

THE OLMECS

The Olmec civilization flourished between about 1200 and 200 B.C. Its legacy to other cultures in Mesoamerica included platform mounds, plazas, ball-courts, and hieroglyphic writing. Olmec artifacts have been found in many parts of Mesoamerica. Olmec art is naturalistic and symbolic. This figurine seems to represent a bald-headed baby.

Facial features similar to peoples of Southeast Asia

Zapotec nobleman trying on jeweled headdress in a detail from a painting by Diego Rivera, called "Cultivation of Maize".

ZAPOTEC CIVILIZATION

The Zapotecs, with their capital at Monte Alban, were established about 600 B.C.; they declined about A.D. 800. The Zapotec state was one of the largest at the time in Mesoamerica. The Zapotecs excelled in the art of featherwork and manufacturing gold jewelry.

Olmec figurine of a bald-headed baby

The Incas and their ancestors

NAZCA
The Nazca inhabited the southern coastal valleys of Peru from 300 B.C. to A.D. 600 and were well known for their arts, which included textiles and metalwork. However, the hallmark of the Nazca civilization is its painted pottery, decorated with realistic and mythological scenes.

BEFORE THE INCA empire reached its peak in South America, many Andean cultures had already laid the framework for its success. These cultures left no written records of their history, and all that is known of them comes from the study of their architecture, pottery, and the remains found in their graves. Archaeologists have identified separate periods of cultural growth, culminating with the Incas. The first complex societies were formed about 1800 B.C. Between this time and the rise of the Incas in the mid-15th century, various cultures emerged, gradually becoming highly organized civilizations with social structures, political and economic systems, specialized artisans, and a religion in which many gods were worshiped. Along the desert coast of Peru there were civilized states such as the Nazca, the Moche, and the Chimu. In the highlands, the Huari and the Tiahuanaco were highly organized cultures. Between A.D. 1438 and 1534, aspects of all these cultures were brought together and refined under the Inca empire.

INCA NOBLES
The scenes painted on vessels and other objects help us learn more about Andean life and culture. For example, Inca nobles usually carried a lance, as this painting on a *kero* or wooden cup, shows.

MOCHE
The Moche people flourished on the northern desert coast of Peru between about the time of Christ and A.D. 600. They were skilled goldsmiths and weavers, and remarkable potters. Their representations of people, plants, animals, and gods in a wide range of activities give us an insight into their lives.

Moche person of high status wearing headband with jaguar decoration and earplugs

TIAHUANACO
The Tiahuanaco empire in the Peruvian highlands flourished between about A.D. 500 and 650. It was a strong state with an impressive ceremonial center.

Tiahuanaco clay jaguar

HUARI
The Huari (A.D. 500 to 900) were neighbors of the Tiahuanaco. Theirs was a highly organized state, with an advanced irrigation system and a distinctive architectural style. It expanded by conquering neighboring areas. Many Huari ideas, such as pottery techniques, were adopted by other Andean cultures. The Huari had their own art style. A common theme is an "angel" figure with wings such as this one.

The Tiahuanaco and the Huari art styles shared many symbols, especially of the cat family

THE CHANCAY

Chancay was a small kingdom that flourished between around A.D. 900 and 1476. It is named after a town on the central coast of Peru. The Chancay had unique styles of architecture and of crafts such as weaving and ceramics. Chancay artisans produced a distinctive type of pottery, such as this figurine in the shape of a woman with her arms outstretched.

Eyes decorated with lines

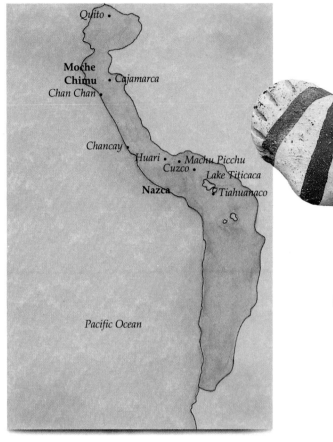

THE INCA EMPIRE *(TAHUANTINSUYU)*

The Inca empire, with its capital at Cuzco, covered a large portion of South America in the 15th and the first quarter of the 16th century. The empire stretched for some 2,500 miles (4,000 km) down the west coast of South America, and covered coastal desert, high mountains, and low-lying jungle. It covered most of modern-day Peru, part of Ecuador and Bolivia, northwest Argentina, and the greater part of Chile.

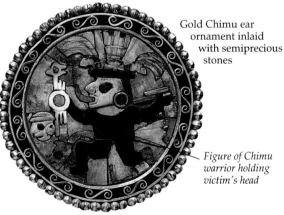
Gold Chimu ear ornament inlaid with semiprecious stones

Figure of Chimu warrior holding victim's head

THE CHIMU

The vast Chimu empire (A.D. 1000 to 1470) had a magnificent capital at Chan Chan, in the same coastal area where the Moche lived. The Chimu were conquered by the Incas. Theirs was an organized culture, with skilled architects. These gold ear ornaments are an example of the sophistication of Chimu goldsmiths.

Chancay figurine with outstretched arms

Farming

AGRICULTURE WAS A VITAL PART of life in pre-Columbian times. Farmers used sophisticated methods of cultivation, and by the time of the Spanish conquest (p. 62) the ancient Americans were the greatest plant cultivators in the world. Maize from Mesoamerica and potatoes from the Andes (pp. 24–25) were some of their contributions to the European diet. Human labor was the vital ingredient in both regions, as there were no animals for carrying loads or plows in Mesoamerica. The Andean people had only the llama, which could carry very small loads. Farming methods varied depending on the climate and geography of the area. For the Aztecs, the most productive crops were grown on the *chinampas*, plots of land built in swampy lakes.

GODDESS OF AGRICULTURE
This incense burner (used to burn a resin called *copal*) represents an agricultural goddess. Agricultural goddesses were often adorned with a pleated paper fan, like this one.

BUILDING *CHINAMPAS* *below*
Chinampas were made by staking out narrow, rectangular strips in marshy lakes. Narrow canals were built between them for canoes to pass along. Each *chinampa* was built up with layers of thick water vegetation cut from the surface of the lake and mud from the bottom of the lake. They were piled up like mats to make the plots. Willow trees were planted around the edge of each *chinampa* to make it more secure.

FERTILE PLOTS
Crops of vegetables and flowers were grown on the fertile *chinampas*, as well as medicinal plants and herbs.

Rich earth from the bottom of the lake was used as fertilizer

Maize

Long broad blade

DIGGING STICK
Digging sticks were made with the strongest and longest-lasting woods.

FARMER'S TOOL
The digging stick, or _uictli,_ was the essential farmer's tool. Digging sticks were used for various jobs, such as hoeing and planting.

PLANTING THE SEED
This illustration from the Codex Florentino shows an Aztec farmer planting maize using a digging stick.

HARVEST TIME
Life in Mesoamerica and in the Andes revolved around the cycles of planting, cultivating, and harvesting crops such as maize.

MAIZE CROP
Maize was the staple food of the Mayans as well as the Aztecs. It is still an important crop today.

Stone head

Wooden handle

AX
Axes were used for chopping or as hammers.

Nazca pot showing a farmer, holding plants

CORNCOB VESSEL
Andean pottery was often made in the shape of the fruit and vegetables that were grown. Maize originated in Mesoamerica, but was widely grown in the Americas.

Head attached to handle with cord

HOE
This tool was used as a spade to turn the soil of the plots.

TERRACES AT MACHU PICCHU
To get the highest yield from their crops, the Incas used sophisticated terracing and irrigation methods on hillsides in the highlands. Building terraces meant that they could use more land for cultivation, and also help to resist erosion of the land by wind and rain.

TENDING CROPS
In the Andean region cultivating the soil was the basis of life. Farmers tended their crops using simple tools such as a digging stick, a clod breaker, and a hoe.

JADE FISH
People from coastal regions drew inspiration from fish and marine life to decorate pottery and jade objects.

Hunting and fishing

HUNTING AND FISHING were important activities in Mesoamerica and in the Andean regions. Meat and fish were part of the diet, especially in the Andean region, depending on what was available in the area. Animal life in the Andes was most abundant in the high mountains of the north, where large mammals such as vicuñas (wild relatives of the llama) and deer roamed. In Mesoamerica, the largest creatures were the peccary (a relative of the pig) and the deer. These were hunted with bows and arrows. Smaller animals such as rabbits and dogs were caught in nets. Mesoamericans and South Americans fished for anything from shellfish to large fish and sea mammals with nets, harpoons, and by angling. They made hooks from sturdy cactus thorns, shell, and bone. Hooks were also made of copper in South America.

IN THE NET
Catching waterfowl in nets was widespread in Mesoamerica around the lake areas.

FISHING NET
The lake system in and around Tenochtitlán provided people with fish and waterfowl, fresh water for drinking, and irrigation for crops. Sometimes fish were transported in canoes to markets and sold. Many nets in present-day Mexico are similar to those produced by the Aztecs and other Mesoamerican peoples. The most common net used by the Aztecs was bag-shaped like this one, made of fiber from the agave plant.

Net tied to fisherman's back

GONE FISHING
This stirrup-spouted Moche vessel depicts a fisherman rowing on a balsawood raft. This was a typical scene on the Peruvian coast.

FAMILY TRADITION
Many trades, such as fishing, were passed from father to son. Boys were taught to fish at an early age; at the age of 14 they went out fishing alone.

The Aztecs and the Mayas made their canoes from hollowed-out tree trunks

Raft made from woven reeds

REED RAFT
Watercraft were fashioned from reeds because of the shortage of wood in areas where few or no trees grew. This type of raft was – and still is – used high in the Andes around Lake Titicaca and on the coast. Large rafts between 14.5 and 20 ft (4.5 and 6.1 m) long had a wooden mast made of reeds for raising and lowering the sail.

DEER-HUNTING SCENE

This beautiful Maya plate from Yucatán, decorated with black and bright orange paints, shows a lively hunting scene. The hunter at the center has already captured a deer, which he carries draped over his head and back. Surrounding this central image are hunters masked as deer in an attempt to distract the animal they want to catch.

FATAL WEAPON

Slings were used as long-range weapons by hunters as well as Inca soldiers. They were made from braided llama wool. The stone was placed in a small cradle. Held at both ends, the sling was whirled around the head. When one end was released, the stone was projected to its mark with great accuracy. The injury inflicted by the stone could be fatal.

Stone placed in braided wool cradle

Hunter carrying deer

Hunter disguised as prey

A BIRD IN THE HAND

The art of the ancient South American people shows us what their activities were. This wooden cup is painted with a scene of a man hunting birds.

BOW AND ARROW *right*

Bows, arrows, and spear-throwers (below) were weapons used originally in Central Mexico, and later introduced to the Maya area. Along with the javelin and the sling, the bow and arrow were used for hunting animals at long range.

Bow

The Maya caught fish in lagoons using a bow and arrow

Arrow

Arrowhead made from obsidian

NAZCA FOX

This fox was part of the decoration on a Nazca pot. Foxes were usually used to symbolize war, but they were also considered pests and were killed mainly with clubs.

Spear

SPEAR AND SPEARTHROWER

Spears (above) had a fire-hardened tip or a point made of chipped stone or obsidian. They were propelled by a spearthrower, or *atlatl* (below). This was a long piece of wood with a groove down the center.

Spear thrower

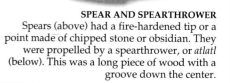

Finger holes for gripping spear thrower

The shaft of the spear rested in this groove

Mesoamerican cities

THE PEOPLES OF MESOAMERICA built their cities in a variety of geographic and climatic areas. Some were built in the highlands, and others in jungles or coastal regions. The Olmecs built their cities in tropical regions, and the people of Teotihuacán, the Toltecs, and the Aztecs, in the highlands. The Mayas built their cities in both highland and lowland regions. These geographical differences influenced the architecture of the cities. As time passed, the cities grew in size. The Olmecs (1200 B.C.) lived in small cities, while Teotihuacán (A.D. 200) had an estimated 150,000 inhabitants or more. The central areas of Mesoamerican cities were reserved for religious and public buildings, and the houses of rulers and of the elite. The houses for the common people were built outside these areas.

CHICHEN ITZA
The Mayan city of Chichén Itzá was built in a strategic place in the center of the Yucatán Peninsula. It became an important commercial center which kept contact with many areas. It is thought that Toltec invaders established themselves there.

Temple-pyramid El Castillo at Chichén Itzá

TRIBUTE TOWNS
The Codex Mendoza (p. 7) gives the names of towns that paid tribute to Tenochtitlán, as well as the goods required. Each of these hieroglyphs (left) represents a subject town.

PALENQUE
This Mayan temple is situated in Palenque, in the midst of tropical jungle. Hidden in the pyramid was the funeral chamber of lord Pacal (p. 53), who ruled for 68 years and was buried in his magnificent resting place in A.D. 683. His sarcophagus contained some of the most beautiful jade objects ever found in Mesoamerica.

Temple of the Inscriptions at Palenque

Shrine to Tlaloc, god of rain

Great temple of the Aztecs

Temple steps

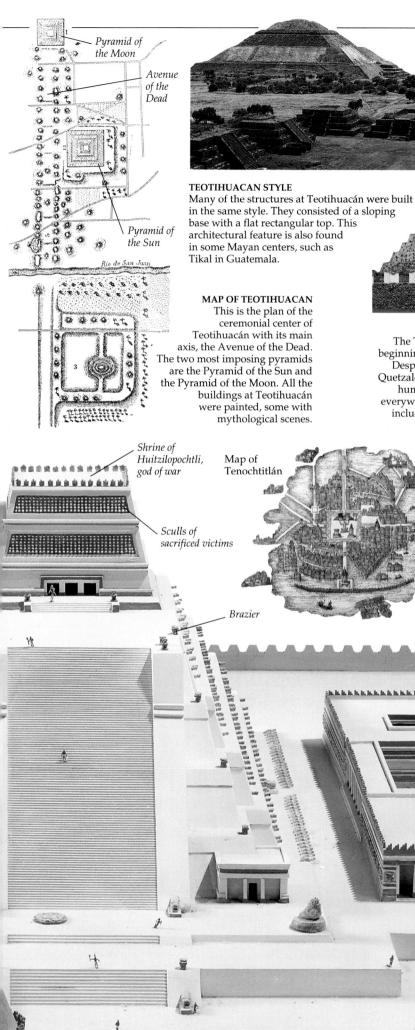

Pyramid of the Moon

Avenue of the Dead

Pyramid of the Sun

Rio de San Juan

TEOTIHUACAN STYLE
Many of the structures at Teotihuacán were built in the same style. They consisted of a sloping base with a flat rectangular top. This architectural feature is also found in some Mayan centers, such as Tikal in Guatemala.

MAP OF TEOTIHUACAN
This is the plan of the ceremonial center of Teotihuacán with its main axis, the Avenue of the Dead. The two most imposing pyramids are the Pyramid of the Sun and the Pyramid of the Moon. All the buildings at Teotihuacán were painted, some with mythological scenes.

TOLTEC WARRIOR
This is one of the warriors on the top of Temple B. These warriors once supported a roof. The warrior is equipped with a spearthrower, and his breastplate in the shape of a butterfly distinguishes him as a warrior.

This temple is known as Temple B, or the Temple of Quetzalcoatl

TULA
The Toltec capital of Tula reflects the beginning of an era of great military action. Despite it being the capital of the god Quetzalcoatl, who was opposed to war and human sacrifice, there are carvings everywhere of warriors equipped for war, including on top of temple pyramids.

Shrine of Huitzilopochtli, god of war

Map of Tenochtitlán

Sculls of sacrificed victims

Brazier

TENOCHTITLAN
This European map of Tenochtitlán, the physical and spiritual heart of the Aztec empire (left), shows the city built on a lake and crossed by four artificial causeways. The conquistadors described the streets as being wide and straight. The Great Temple of the Aztecs (pp. 30–31) was at the center. This model (below) shows the Great Temple inside the sacred precinct. The temple was dedicated to the god of rain as well as the god of war, who was the god of the Aztecs. Just outside the ceremonial center were palaces, warrior schools, shrines, and a ball court (pp. 58–59).

Cities of the Andes

THE PEOPLE OF THE ANDEAN REGION lived in either highland or coastal areas. They built their cities to suit the location, from materials that were locally available. The typical highland building had a sloping thatched roof and stone walls. On the coast, buildings tended to have mud-brick (adobe) walls with painted mud plaster, and flat roofs. Highland cities such as Machu Picchu could not be built on a regular grid plan, in contrast to the cities in flat coastal areas, such as Chan Chan. The first buildings to be lived in as homes date to the 4th century B.C. Public constructions such as government buildings, storehouses, bridges, and canals were built by taxpayers as a kind of labor tax, with the state providing the materials.

INCA STONEMASONS
The Incas are renowned for their fine stonework. Huge stone blocks were cut by masons using just a stone hammer, and wet sand to polish them. The blocks fitted so closely that no mortar was needed.

OLLANTAYTAMBO
The Inca town of Ollantaytambo has some of the most impressive architectural remains in Peru. This doorway was built with rectangular blocks of stone. Each stone was precisely cut and fitted to a specific position.

TIAHUANACO
The city of Tiahuanaco (p. 10) is situated on a high plain nearly 13,100 ft (4,000 m) above sea level, rimmed by the mountains of the Andes. The stunning architecture of its ceremonial center included an impressive number of stone sculptures. The Gateway of the Sun (above) was carved from a single block of stone. A carving above the doorway portrays a sun god.

Bird motif on adobe wall of compound, Chan Chan

ADOBE DECORATION
The Chimu decorated their thick adobe (mud) walls with molded animals, usually associated with the sea – birds, fish, and men in boats.

Royal compound at Chan Chan, capital of the Chimu kingdom

CHAN CHAN
The Chimu people built urban centers; Chan Chan, the coastal capital of the Chimu empire, is a good example of this. The city was organized on a grid plan, and covered approximately 2.3 sq mi (6 sq km). It contained ten compounds, each enclosed by a high adobe (mud) wall. These are thought to be the royal residences and administrative centers of Chimu kings. Each king lived, died, and was buried in his secluded compound.

European map of Cuzco

Stone walls of Sacsahuaman fort

CUZCO

The religious and political capital of the Incas is situated at the heart of the Andes with the mountains encircling it. The town was divided into sections by narrow paved streets, designed to represent the four quarters of the Inca empire. It had ceremonial plazas, palaces, and temples. Only the rulers and nobility lived in the city center. This European drawing wrongly portrays Cuzco as a walled town. Much of Cuzco was destroyed by the Spanish, who built their city on Inca ruins.

SACSAHUAMAN FORT

Cuzco was protected from the enemy by the fortress of Sacsahuaman, built on a steep hill overlooking the city from the north. The fort was built with locally quarried stone, and each giant block was individually shaped. These three impressive stone walls – standing 52 ft (16 m) – guarded the fortress.

INCA BATHS

Inca palaces sometimes had sunken stone baths for the kings to relax and bathe in. Water ran along stone channels into the bath. These baths at Tambo Machay, near Cuzco, were built at the site of a sacred spring. They were used by the Inca kings.

Machu Picchu

Inca baths at Tambo Machay

MACHU PICCHU

Strategically positioned on the edge of the Inca empire, the remote city of Machu Picchu was probably built at the end of the 15th century. It was not discovered by the Spanish conquistadors, nor by other Westerners until 1911. The site is an outstanding example of Inca architecture – a natural fortress protected by steep slopes, surrounded by high mountain peaks, and approachable from only one point. Of its 143 granite buildings, about 80 were houses, the rest being ceremonial buildings such as temples. Many mummies were found at Machu Picchu, most of them of women.

COUPLE EMBRACING
In both Mesoamerica and the Andean region, a wife's role was to obey her husband. Even in art, women were often depicted in a passive position, and men in a more active position. This Mayan clay statue shows a man embracing a woman. Both wear elaborate headdresses, earplugs, and necklaces, which indicate that they were wealthy.

Figure has eyes and teeth inlaid with shell.

Family life

T HE MESOAMERICAN MAN, as a husband and father, was responsible for the well-being of his household. He was expected to support his family, as well as his government, through hard work and by paying taxes. The woman, as a wife and mother, devoted her time and energy to running her household and caring for her children. Girls were taught domestic chores such as weaving and cooking, and sons followed their fathers while they worked. Children had free schooling, and nobles had their own schools. Family life was similar in the Andean region. The father worked to support the family and pay taxes; the mother worked in the home, helped her husband with his work, and cared for the children. Inca commoners had to educate their own children.

Aztec couple during marriage ceremony

JUST MARRIED
One of the rituals in an Aztec wedding ceremony was to tie the young man's cloak and the girl's blouse together. The wedding party followed, with dancing and singing.

FERTILE BLESSING
Both the Mesoamericans and the Incas considered it important for a married couple to have children. The Aztecs worshiped goddesses of fertility. This wooden Aztec sculpture is of a young woman dressed in a skirt and bare-breasted. She may be a goddess of fertility.

Stirrup handle

CELEBRATION
There were great celebrations when an Aztec baby was born. They lasted for days, during which astrologers checked to see when would be a favorable day for the baby to be named.

Woman giving birth, helped by two women

CHILDBIRTH SCENE
Women in the Andes were helped in childbirth by women who had given birth to twins, as well as by neighbors. There were no midwives. After birth the mother and baby washed in a river. The umbilical cord was not thrown away, but was kept in the house.

BRINGING UP BABIES
Family scenes are common in Aztec art, and show women performing various activities. This woman is carrying two children, one under each arm. One of the main roles of an Aztec woman was to bring up her children until they were ready to leave home and marry.

Steam made by throwing water on walls of bathhouse

Fire for heating steam bath

STEAM BATHS

Bathing was a part of the daily family routine of the Aztecs, both for keeping clean and for purification. Almost every home had a steam bath alongside it. The bathhouse was a small building that was heated by a fireplace. When water was thrown on the hot inside walls, the room filled with steam.

WOMAN CARRYING LOAD

The duties of women in the Andean region varied according to their rank. The woman depicted in this Moche vessel was probably a commoner's wife and was expected to help her husband when necessary. This included carrying heavy loads on her back. She wears a strap that passes around her forehead to hold the load on her back.

Strap around forehead

PUNISHMENT

From the age of 11 years, disobedient Aztec children were punished in various ways by their parents. Punishments included pricking their skin with spines and making them inhale chili smoke by holding them over a fire with chili peppers.

CHILD'S PLAY

Until they reached an age where they had to help their parents with their work, young children played in and around the home. This clay "toy" is in the form of a dog on wheels. "Toys" such as this one show that the Mesoamericans knew about the wheel. However, they used it for decorative purposes only. They did not use the wheel for practical purposes, such as on wagons to help them carry loads. "Toys" with wheels have been found mainly in graves in parts of the Gulf of Mexico. Toys in the form of dogs may have been thought to help the soul of the deceased to find his or her resting place in the afterlife.

Collar

Wheel turns on bolt

WATER GOURD

Maize cob used as cork

The gourd, a vegetable with a hard shell, was frequently used as a container after being dried out. Gourds were mainly used for carrying water. This type of gourd grows in most parts of the Americas.

At home

Sharp wooden teeth

HANDY TOOL

Combs were made of bone or wood. They were used for hairdressing and, in South America, for preparing wool. Some were even used to make patterns on pottery.

THE AZTECS, MAYAS, AND INCAS lived in simple houses, many with only one main room and very little furniture. Inca houses were made of stone blocks or of mud (adobe), while most Aztec and Mayan houses were made of adobe. For the Aztecs, furniture was simply a few beds made of reed mats. There were also low tables, and reed chests for clothes. The Aztec home had an inside courtyard with a kitchen, and a small shrine to the gods. The bathroom was in a separate building. The homes of wealthy nobles and dignitaries had more rooms, more elaborate furniture, and a bigger garden.

INSIDE AN AZTEC HOUSE
An Aztec woman's home meant almost everything to her. She spent most of her day in the house, looking after the children, cooking, or weaving.

MULTIPURPOSE POT
This pot was used to store liquids and food. It was often kept upright with a ring made of reeds.

REED MAT
In Mesoamerica people sat, played, and slept on reed mats. This type of mat would have been used as a "rug" on the floor of most houses. It is thinner than the mats used as "beds." Both the rich and poor had mats such as this one.

Bowl has three sturdy legs

TRIPOD BOWL
Potters working in Teotihuacán often made three-legged bowls like this, sometimes with a lid. Everyday pots were usually plain, but others had a pattern cut into the surface, or painted on like this one.

Inca doors and windows were shaped like a trapezoid: four-sided, but with only two parallel sides

INCA HOUSE
The most common type of Inca house, whether made from adobe (mud) or stone, was rectangular with a thatched roof, and usually had just one room. There was no furniture in an Inca house. The stone blocks used to build houses were carved so that that they fitted together perfectly, and there was no need for cement.

CURVED KNIFE
Knives of various shapes, with metal blades, were known as *tumi*. This Peruvian *tumi* is made of copper with a fitted bone handle.

Curved blade may have been used for cutting up food

End of handle is in the shape of an animal's head

Chisel has a wooden handle carved in the shape of a jaguar

HOW PEOPLE LIVED
This pot was found in an ancient Peruvian grave. It is an elaborate, decorated version of the type of pot that would have been used in the Andean region for everyday cooking and eating. Objects like this pot, found in graves, give us an idea of how people lived.

JAGUAR CHISEL
Everyday Andean tools, such as this chisel, have been found in *huacas* or sacred places.

GRINDING STONE
Early every morning, the women would revive the hearth fire and grind maize on the *metlatl* or grinding stone (made of volcanic stone, usually basalt). Grinding stones were basic tools in the kitchen. Today, grinding stones are still used throughout the Mesoamerican region, mainly for grinding maize into flour.

Cylindrical stone used to press the maize against the grinding stone

Vessels with stirrup spouts such as this one were made only in South America

This water pot is in the shape of a Mochica building

HIGH-CLASS VESSEL
In the Andean region, a person's status could be told by the kind of drinking vessel he or she used. Peasants drank from gourd bowls, while the well--to-do drank from clay containers such as this one. Some wealthy people drank from gold or silver vessels.

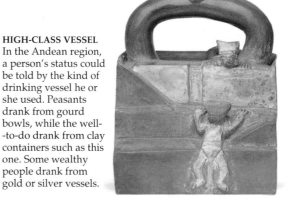

Food and drink

Guinea pig meat was the only meat regularly eaten by the Andeans.

Chocolate was made with ground cacao beans and water

THE MESOAMERICANS AND ANDEANS ate simply. Maize was the central food in their diet, supplemented by other vegetables, such as beans and squashes, grown in both regions. Not all foods were grown in both regions, however. Potatoes and quinoa (a grain) came from the Andean region, while avocados and tomatoes were mainly consumed in Mesoamerica, along with all kinds of fruit. Maize was made into a sort of porridge called *atole* in Mesoamerica and *capia* in Inca territory. Maize cakes were often eaten in both regions, but only the Mesoamerican peoples ate maize *tortillas* (pancakes) with every meal. A favorite dish among Aztecs and Incas was *tamales*, a kind of envelope of steamed maize stuffed with vegetables or meat. In Mesoamerica the main meal was eaten during the hottest part of the day. In both regions, it was customary for everyone to eat twice a day.

CACAO
A chocolate drink made from cacao was drunk by wealthy Mesoamericans. It was sweetened with honey and flavored with vanilla.

Cacao pod

Bowl-shaped stone mortar

Club-shaped pestle

MORTAR AND PESTLE
Chilies and tomatoes were used for making sauces. They were crushed with a stone called a pestle in a mortar, which was a carved cylindrical stone with three little feet.

GRIDDLE WITH *TORTILLAS*
Once the *tortillas* have been made, they are cooked over the fire on a clay disk called a *comal*. *Tortillas* are still the central part of the Mesoamerican diet.

WOMEN PREPARING MAIZE
The preparation of maize was a daily task for the Mesoamerican housewife. This section of a painting by Mexican artist Diego Rivera shows a woman grinding the corn kernels into flour between a stone roller and slab. The flour is made into a dough, which another woman pats into *tortillas*.

Comal

LLAMA
The tender meat of the llama was eaten by the Incas and their ancestors. However, they ate it with moderation, as the llama was useful in many other ways.

Llama tied up with ropes

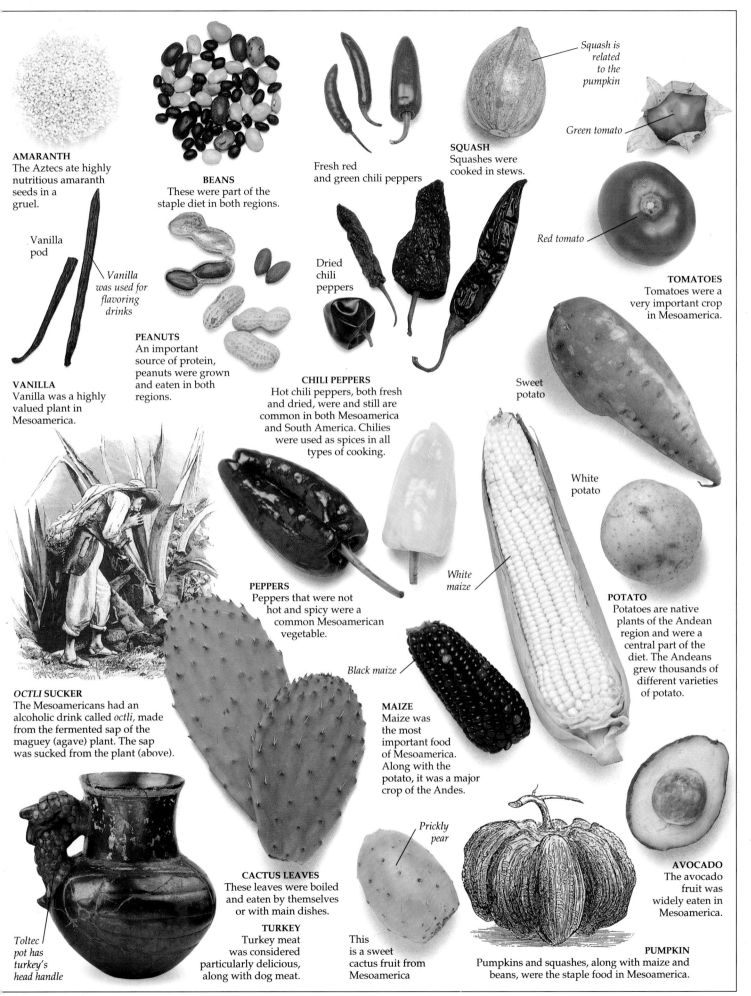

AMARANTH
The Aztecs ate highly nutritious amaranth seeds in a gruel.

Vanilla pod

Vanilla was used for flavoring drinks

VANILLA
Vanilla was a highly valued plant in Mesoamerica.

BEANS
These were part of the staple diet in both regions.

PEANUTS
An important source of protein, peanuts were grown and eaten in both regions.

Fresh red and green chili peppers

Dried chili peppers

CHILI PEPPERS
Hot chili peppers, both fresh and dried, were and still are common in both Mesoamerica and South America. Chilies were used as spices in all types of cooking.

SQUASH
Squashes were cooked in stews.

Squash is related to the pumpkin

Green tomato

Red tomato

TOMATOES
Tomatoes were a very important crop in Mesoamerica.

Sweet potato

White potato

PEPPERS
Peppers that were not hot and spicy were a common Mesoamerican vegetable.

White maize

Black maize

MAIZE
Maize was the most important food of Mesoamerica. Along with the potato, it was a major crop of the Andes.

POTATO
Potatoes are native plants of the Andean region and were a central part of the diet. The Andeans grew thousands of different varieties of potato.

OCTLI **SUCKER**
The Mesoamericans had an alcoholic drink called *octli*, made from the fermented sap of the maguey (agave) plant. The sap was sucked from the plant (above).

Prickly pear

Toltec pot has turkey's head handle

CACTUS LEAVES
These leaves were boiled and eaten by themselves or with main dishes.

TURKEY
Turkey meat was considered particularly delicious, along with dog meat.

This is a sweet cactus fruit from Mesoamerica

AVOCADO
The avocado fruit was widely eaten in Mesoamerica.

PUMPKIN
Pumpkins and squashes, along with maize and beans, were the staple food in Mesoamerica.

CODEX TRIBUTE
The goods paid as tribute to the Aztec rulers were recorded in books such as the Codex Mendoza.

Pottery bowl

Simple cotton blankets

Heavily decorated cotton blankets

Bundle of copal incense

Pots of honey

Bin with maize and chia seeds

IN MESOAMERICA and in the Andean region, it was the commoners who mainly supported the state by paying taxes. People of high rank did not pay taxes, nor did the sick and disabled, for example. In Inca territory, each province had to pay specific amounts of tribute to the government. At Tenochtitlán, the Aztec capital, the residents of each borough belonged to an institution called a *calpulli*, whose leader made sure that taxes were paid. Goods of all kinds were exchanged in both regions, and in Mesoamerica all the products of the land were sold in busy marketplaces. Aztec merchants went on long expeditions to distant lands to trade for such items as tropical feathers, gold, fine stones, and jaguar skins.

RUNNER
This Moche pot depicts a runner. Runners, or *chasquis*, ran from one place to the next, usually carrying messages. The Incas had an excellent road system, which was essential for controlling the empire, for trade, and for communication.

THE SALE OF MAIZE
Much can be learned from the murals of Diego Rivera about how the ancient Mexicans lived. Rivera, one of the most remarkable modern Mexican muralists, was well-read about life in Tenochtitlán. This detail of a busy market scene shows women selling various types of maize.

Jaguar headdress

WARRIOR'S SUIT AND SHIELD
Tunics and shields were very expensive items of tribute. Tunics were either made of feather-covered material or of animal pelts. The jaguar helmet (left) was the warrior's insignia as well as his protection. According to the Codex Mendoza, tribute of this kind had to be paid once a year.

Jaguar warrior's suit

Feather shield

Ocelot skin

FUR TRADE
Animal skins were sold in the market at Tlatelolco. The skin of the puma was particularly valued by the Mayas, as its tawny color reminded them of the sun. Jaguar skins were equally valued. The black spots were thought to symbolize the night sky. Jaguar skins were used as seats for the rulers, as book covers, and as cloaks.

Puma skin

Jaguar skin

TLATELOLCO MARKET
When the Spanish arrived in Mexico, they found that the market at Tlatelolco (the sister city of Tenochtitlán) was bigger and better stocked than any market in Spain. Supervisors regulated prices, and judges were present in case of disputes or theft. Much of the buying and selling was done by barter – exchanging products – although copper axes sometimes served as money in both Mesoamerica and the Andes.

Inca treasurer records goods in storehouses on *quipu*.

Cacao beans

Melon seeds

Quetzal feather

Ax heads

Jade beads

Tropical bird feather

TRADING

Items such as cacao beans and feathers were in great demand, as vast quantities of each were used to pay tribute. The merchants from Tenochtitlán and neighboring major cities exported and traded luxury objects made from imported raw materials or materials obtained by tribute. In return for their goods they obtained other goods such as tropical feathers (especially quetzal feathers), cacao beans, animal skins, and gold.

Storing agricultural produce in government granaries

INCA STOREHOUSES *left*

The Incas kept all kinds of supplies in storehouses used by government officials and those who were in need due to an illness, or after a crisis or a siege. They kept them full of items such as weapons, cloth, wool, potatoes, and maize.

All the pottery stalls were placed together in the market

Simply decorated clay vessel for everyday use

Simple clay bowl

The market was a place where people exchanged news and goods

27

The warrior

WARFARE was a normal part of life in both Mesoamerica and the Inca region of South America, and city-states frequently fought each other. In Mesoamerica, youths had to join the army at the age of 17 for a period of intensive training. The Inca and Mesoamerican peoples were educated in the arts of war, and the fighting spirit was encouraged. Among the Aztecs the best and most common way to climb the social ladder was by showing courage in battle. One of the main aims of going to war was to capture enemy warriors for sacrifice. Aztec warriors were in a constant "sacred war," as they believed that human sacrifice kept the sun in motion (pp. 36–37). Both the Incas and the Aztecs added newly conquered areas to their empires. As power and wealth grew, they developed a thirst for more conquests that would enrich the state and add to the glory of the emperor.

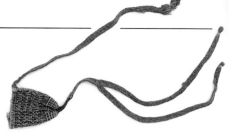

Slings like this Peruvian Chancay woven one, made from wool and cotton, were used in warfare. Warriors used stones as missiles.

TOLTEC WARRIOR
This sculpture shows a richly attired Toltec warrior wearing a feather headdress, earplugs, and a butterfly breastplate. In one hand he carries an *atlatl*, or spearthrower, and in the other a sheaf of darts.

CAPTURED
Aztec warriors who took captives were awarded costumes with distinctive designs, such as jaguar costumes and mantles. The more captives they took, the more elaborate was the costume.

Flint knife has a sharp serrated edge

AZTEC WEAPONS
A warrior usually carried spears of wood, with the blade edged with chert or obsidian, and a *maquahuitl* or war club made of wood, also, which was about 30 in (76 cm) in length. It had grooved sides set with sharp obsidian blades. Warriors also carried stabbing javelins and round shields with protective feather fringes. Flint and obsidian knives such as these (left) were also used for human sacrifices.

Club

Long, razor-sharp knife made from obsidian

OBSIDIAN WOODEN CLUB *below*
One of the main weapons used by the Aztecs was a *maquahuitl*, a wooden club edged with obsidian blades. Obsidian is a volcanic glass that is sharp enough to sever a horse's head.

EFFIGY POT
The Moche culture from the north coast of Peru often depicted warriors, such as this warrior holding a club, on clay vessels. Shields were often shown strapped to the wrist.

OBSIDIAN SPEAR *below*
A warrior usually carried one or two throwing spears of wood, the blades edged with flakes of sharp stone capable of inflicting deep cuts.

Obsidian blades around edge of spear

MONTEZUMA'S STONE
This sculpted stone depicts the battles of the Aztec ruler Montezuma I. The top of the stone was used for gladiatorial fights. It also served as a vessel for the hearts of sacrificial victims and other offerings. This detail (left) symbolizes the capture and incorporation of a city into the Aztec empire.

TERRACOTTA EAGLE WARRIOR
The most prestigious military orders were those of the eagle and the jaguar. These warriors wore either eagle or jaguar costumes. This life-size sculpture represents an eagle warrior. It is one of a pair that was found flanking a doorway to the chamber where the eagle warriors met, next to the Great Temple of the Aztecs in Tenochtitlán. The eagle was the symbol of the sun, to whom all sacrifices were offered.

Helmet shaped like an eagle's beak

The Aztec Warrior

The ideal Aztec warrior was noble and brave, and had to serve and respect the gods. Warriors were so important in Aztec Mexico that the Aztec ruler had to start his rule on the battlefield, adding cities and provinces to the empire, and capturing prisoners for ritual sacrifice, an essential part of the Aztec religion.

The eagle warrior's costume has wings on the arms, to imitate the eagle

Imitation talons

FEATHER SHIELD
All Aztec warriors carried a shield for protection. This one is made of jaguar skin and bright tropical feathers. Featherworkers were responsible for making shields, headdresses, fans, and other objects. Some of these were made of turkey and duck feathers, but many of the valuable objects were made of bright green quetzal feathers.

TEMPLE WARRIOR
This watercolor painting is of a warrior figure that decorated the doorway of a temple in the Mayan city Chichén Itzá. The warrior is dressed and armed in a fashion similar to that of Toltec warriors, as Toltec influence was great in some Mayan territories. He wears a shield around his waist, protective bands on one arm and on his legs, and is carrying spears.

Religious life

RELIGION TOUCHED almost every aspect of Mesoamerican and Inca life. One of the many focal points for the religious rites was sacred buildings, or temples, dedicated to the gods. In the Andean region people worshiped a variety of shrines and objects and the natural forces associated with them, known as *huacas*. The Aztecs also worshiped sacred places. Within the official Inca state religion the sun was the most important god. It was a dominant force and a symbol of prestige and power. The Incas worshiped the sun mainly so that they would have abundant crops. The Aztec religion was also concerned with the sun. The Aztecs believed that they lived in the era of the fifth sun and that one day the world would end violently. In order to postpone their destruction, men performed human sacrifices. Their duty was to feed the gods with human blood, thereby keeping the sun alive.

Codex illustration of an Aztec temple at Tenochtitlán

TEMPLE OF THE GIANT JAGUAR
To worship their gods, the Mayans built magnificent ceremonial centers filled with temples, courts, and plazas. This majestic temple in Tikal stands in the middle of its ceremonial center. It is a giant temple-pyramid with nine sloping terraces. The ornamental roof comb perched on the temple roof soars to a height of 161 ft (50 m).

Intihuatana *means "hitching post of the sun"*

STONE OF *INTIHUATANA*
The principal Inca temples for the cult of the sun were built by the government throughout the Inca empire. This stone in Machu Picchu worked as a solar clock and allowed people to calculate the winter solstice (21st of June) for the important festival of the sun god.

Priests performing rituals in a temple during "new fire" ceremony

After sacrifice, bodies of sacrificial victims thrown down stairs

AZTEC "NEW FIRE" CEREMONY
This religious event took place in temples every 52 years. When the day arrived, people extinguished all fires, and discarded idols and household utensils. The new "century" began when the sun's rays appeared again at dawn.

MODEL OF THE GREAT TEMPLE AT TENOCHTITLAN
At the heart of the city of Tenochtitlán was a walled precinct. Within it, sharing a single tall pyramid, were the twin shrines dedicated to Tlaloc, the god of rain, and Huitzilopochtli, god of war and the tribal god of the Aztecs. The Great Temple was the physical and symbolic center of the Aztec world, where human sacrifices and offerings to the Aztec gods took place. Each Aztec ruler tried to make a bigger and more impressive new temple. This model shows the many temples that were built, one above the other. The oldest, inner temple has a chacmool (a statue with a receptacle for hearts and blood) on the left and a sacrificial stone on the right. The excavators of the site found more than 6,000 objects buried as offerings to Tlaloc and Huitzilopochtli.

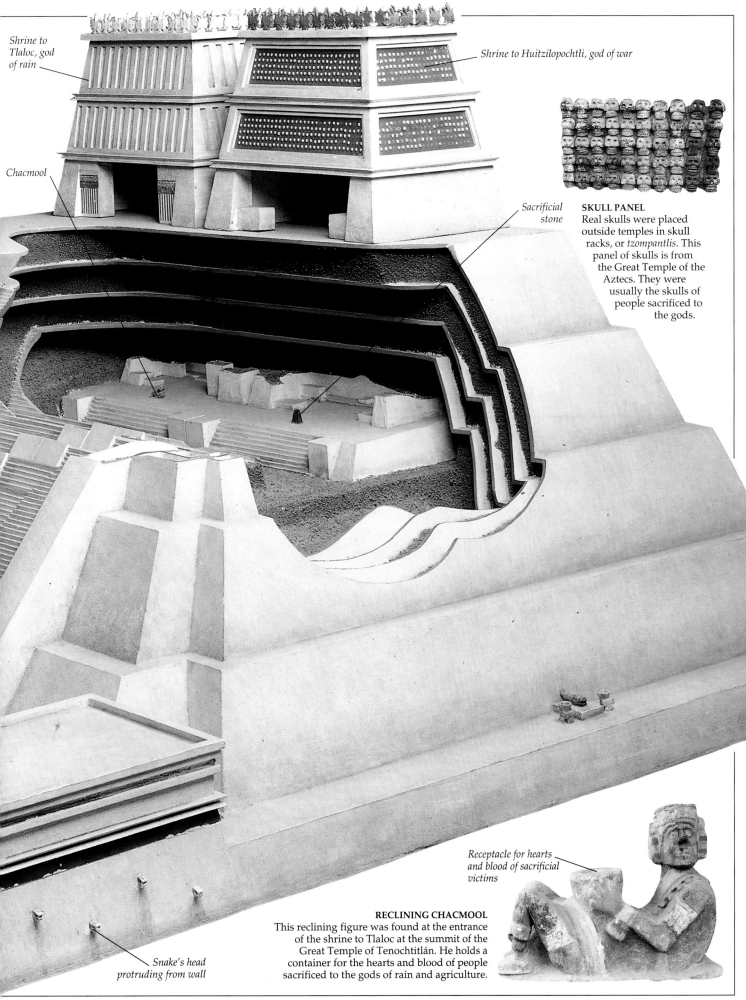

Shrine to
Tlaloc, god
of rain

Shrine to Huitzilopochtli, god of war

Chacmool

Sacrificial
stone

SKULL PANEL
Real skulls were placed
outside temples in skull
racks, or *tzompantlis*. This
panel of skulls is from
the Great Temple of the
Aztecs. They were
usually the skulls of
people sacrificed to
the gods.

Receptacle for hearts
and blood of sacrificial
victims

RECLINING CHACMOOL
This reclining figure was found at the entrance
of the shrine to Tlaloc at the summit of the
Great Temple of Tenochtitlán. He holds a
container for the hearts and blood of people
sacrificed to the gods of rain and agriculture.

Snake's head
protruding from wall

31

Gods and goddesses

Aztec god from Codex Florentino

THE MESOAMERICAN and Inca people both worshiped many gods. They had similar religions – based mainly on the worship of agricultural gods – even though the gods' names and the symbols for them were different. People asked their gods for good crops and good health or for their welfare. The main Inca god was the creator god Viracocha. His assistants were the gods of the sun, moon, stars, and thunder, as well as the gods of the earth and the sea. As farming occupied such an important place in both regions, the "earth mother," or earth goddess, was particularly important. The Aztecs adopted many gods from other civilizations. As with the Incas, each god was connected with some aspect of nature or natural force.

God of springtime, wearing the skin of a sacrificial victim

RAIN GOD
Many Mesoamerican vessels and sculptures are associated with Tlaloc, the god of rain and agricultural fertility. It is likely that this water vessel depicts the face of the god of rain, as it contains the vital liquid necessary to fertilize the earth.

Tlaloc had "goggle eyes"

GOD OF THE SPRINGTIME
The Aztec god of the springtime and of vegetation was called Xipe Totec (Our Flayed Lord). He was also the patron of metal workers. The victims sacrificed in honor of this god were flayed (skinned alive). After flaying the victim, priests would wear the victim's skin. This symbolized the annual spring renewal of vegetation – in other words, the renewal of the "earth's skin."

Xipe Totec, god of springtime and of vegetation

Feathered serpent, Quetzalcoatl

Rain god, Tlaloc

Reconstruction of temple of Quetzalcoatl in Teotihuacán

GOD OF NATURE
Quetzalcoatl, whose name means feathered serpent, was a god of nature – of the air, and of earth. The temple of Quetzalcoatl at Teotihuacán is decorated with large sculptures of feathered serpents, as this reconstruction shows.

Chicomecoatl wore a four-sided paper headdress with pleated rosettes at the corners

AZTEC MAIZE GODDESSES
There were three goddesses associated with maize. This statue is of Chicomecoatl, the goddess of mature maize. This was the best seed corn of the harvest, which was put away for sowing. There was also a goddess of tender maize, and one who was the personification of the maize plant.

Double maize cobs

WAR GOD
Huitzilopochtli (the Hummingbird of the left) was the tribal god of the Aztecs. In this illustration we see him armed with his serpent of fire and his shield.

GOD OF THE DEAD
Mictlantecuhtli was god of the dead in Aztec Mexico. Those who died a natural death went to the Mictlan, where he lived, in the cold and infernal region of the fleshless.

The Inca people worshiped the moon and the sun

SEPTEMBER FESTIVAL
The Incas celebrated different religious festivities every month of the year. Here we see the celebrations for September dedicated to female goddesses. This festivity was celebrated under the protection of the moon and the sun gods.

WORSHIPING THE SUN
The Incas worshiped the sun, Inti. Most agricultural religions included worship of both the sun and the rain, as they are both essential for good harvests. The sun was the most important god of the Inca royal dynasty. Inca kings believed that they were descendants of Inti.

Gold disk

SKY OR MOON GOD
The handle of this Peruvian ceremonial knife is decorated with the image of either the sky or the moon god. His arms are opened wide, and he is holding two disks. He wears a beautiful filigree headdress with turquoise inlay.

Turquoise was used for the inlays of the eyes, necklace, earplugs, and the clothing

Chac carries a bowl in his right hand and a ball of smoking incense in his left.

MAYA GOD OF RAIN
The Maya god of rain was called Chac. One of the sacrifices in honor of this god was to drown children in wells. In some Maya regions the god of rain was so important that the facades of buildings were covered with masks of Chac.

Chancay "doll" found in grave

Life after death

THE PEOPLE OF Mesoamerica and South America believed that after they died they would go on living in another world. They were buried with goods of all descriptions that would be of use to them. By studying the goods found in graves, pre-Hispanic codices, and early colonial manuscripts, archaeologists have pieced together some of the beliefs about death and the afterlife. It was the way that Aztecs died, rather than the way they lived, that decided what would happen to them in the afterlife. If a person died a normal death, his or her soul had to pass through the nine levels of the underworld before reaching Mictlan, the realm of the death god. Warriors who died in battle and women who died in childbirth, however, joined the sun god in the sky.

ALL WRAPPED UP
Many mummy bundles such as this one have been discovered in the Andean region. The corpse was placed in a flexed position and bound with cord to help maintain the pose. It was then wrapped in textiles and seated upright. Goods were placed around the mummy in the grave.

DOLL COMPANION
Colorful figures found in Chancay tombs, such as this one, are called "dolls" because it is believed that they were used in daily life. They were placed with the deceased to serve them in the afterlife.

Mayan burial urn

MUMMY OF DEAD KING
In Andean society, mummies were looked after as if they were alive. The living often consulted their dead in important matters. At special festivals, the mummies of emperors were paraded in the streets.

THE RICH AND THE POOR
The more goods that were placed in a grave, the better off the individual was. Wooden figurines such as this one of a man have been found in many Andean tombs. But tombs filled with golden objects, and more elaborately prepared corpses, indicate that everyone was not equal.

MAYAN BURIAL
The Mayas usually buried their dead under house floors or in the ground. Sometimes, however, they cremated the remains or buried them in caves, underground tanks, or urns. The privileged classes were buried in very elaborate tombs. One common type of burial for children was to place the corpse in a large urn, covered by a tripod (three-legged) vessel or pot fragment.

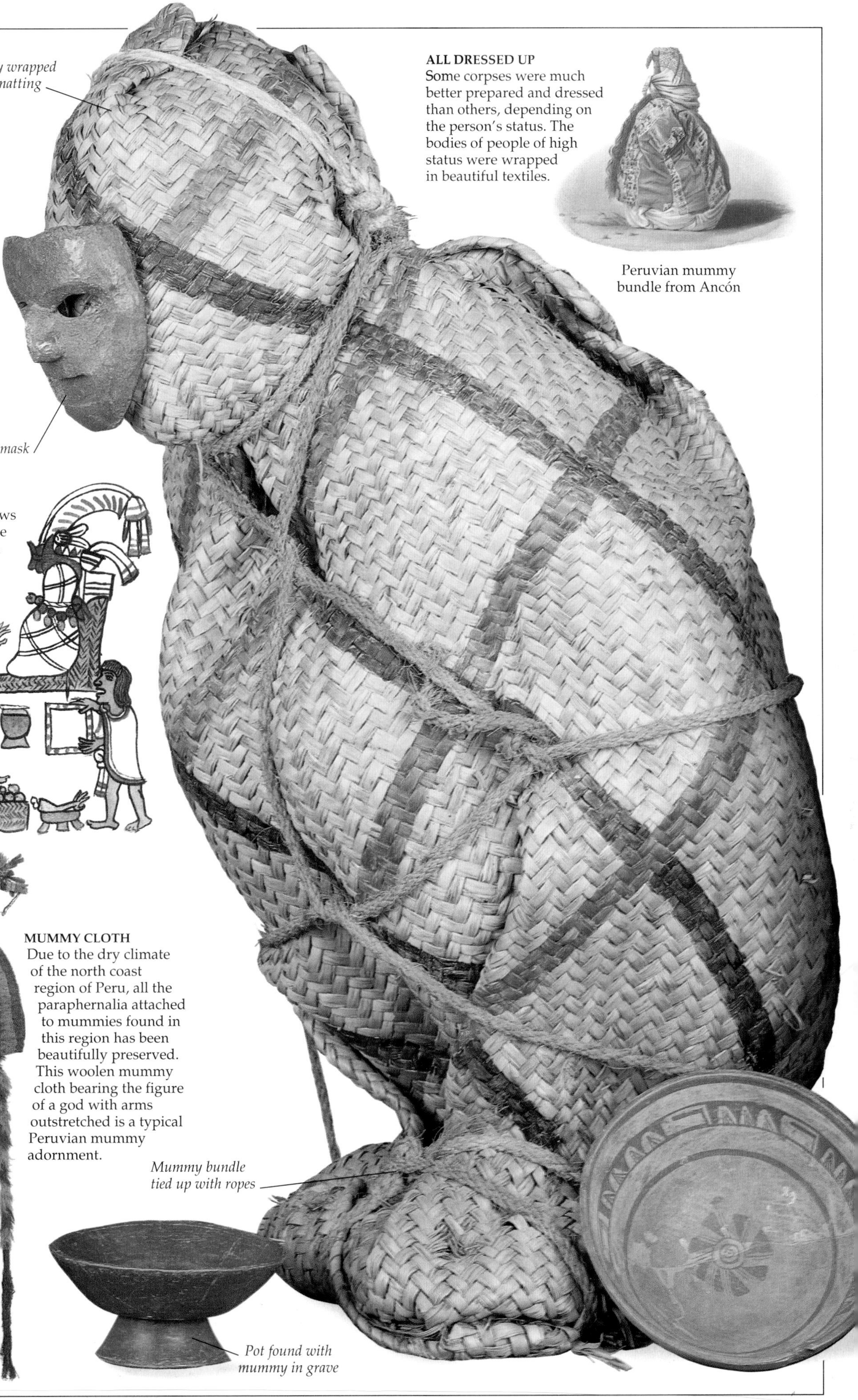

Mummy wrapped in reed matting

MIXTEC MUMMY BUNDLE
Mesoamerican mummies were wrapped in a similar way to those from South America. A mask was attached to the face of the mummy. The mask was usually made of stone but some masks were made of wood. People thought these masks would protect the deceased from the dangers of the afterlife.

Stone mask

RITES OF DEATH
This codex illustration shows an Aztec ritual in which the limbs of a sacrificial victim are being eaten by the victim's captor. This is being carried out in the presence of a mummified body.

MUMMY CLOTH
Due to the dry climate of the north coast region of Peru, all the paraphernalia attached to mummies found in this region has been beautifully preserved. This woolen mummy cloth bearing the figure of a god with arms outstretched is a typical Peruvian mummy adornment.

ALL DRESSED UP
Some corpses were much better prepared and dressed than others, depending on the person's status. The bodies of people of high status were wrapped in beautiful textiles.

Peruvian mummy bundle from Ancón

Mummy bundle tied up with ropes

Pot found with mummy in grave

Human sacrifice

SACRIFICE WAS A RELIGIOUS RITUAL in Mesoamerica and in the Inca region of South America. The Incas and the Aztecs held special ceremonies that involved sacrifice in temples or on mountaintops. The Mayas sometimes sacrificed victims in wells. Priests performed the sacrifices, which took place at important festivals throughout the year. The Incas practiced human sacrifice only in serious crises and for special events. For the Aztecs, sacrifice was more widespread and more frequent. The victims were men, women, and children – and sometimes animals. It was common for the Incas to ritually strangle women, while the Mayas sometimes drowned their victims and the Aztecs removed the victim's heart. Most sacrifices were performed in honor of the sun, rain, and earth gods. Human sacrifice was a communion with the gods: it was necessary to feed them to keep the cosmic order. People believed that just as the gods sacrificed themselves during the creation of the sun and the moon, they had to do the same.

SACRIFICIAL KNIFE
This decorated flint knife was found in the Great Temple of the Aztecs (p. 30–31). Stone knives such as this one were used to kill victims of sacrifice.

Eyes made of shell and pyrite

Skull mask found among the offerings in the Great Temple

Sacrificial knives were probably inserted in the nose and mouth to intimidate enemies

SACRIFICE
The most common form of sacrifice among the Aztecs was to stretch the victim over a sacrificial stone. Five priests took part – four of them held the limbs and one took out the heart.

SKULL MASK
This human skull was probably used as a mask in ritual performances. It may have been the skull of a sacrificial victim.

Illustration from Codex Magliabecchiano

AFTER SACRIFICE
Once an Aztec priest had taken the heart out, it was placed in a receptacle, such as the one below. The victim was then thrown down the temple stairs. The body was picked up and part of it, such as the thigh, was given as a reward to the victim's captor. The Aztecs practiced cannibalism in some religious ceremonies under strict regulations. For example, enemy captives were ritually eaten, but only legs or arms could be consumed.

PRECIOUS HEART
This beautifully carved greenstone heart represents the most precious organ that the Aztecs could offer to their gods. Likewise, jade was considered the most valuable stone and the most precious material, far more so than gold. Jade was the symbol for life and agriculture.

SACRIFICIAL STONES AND VESSELS
This ritual vessel (right) may have been intended to contain the blood or the hearts of sacrificial victims. The outer surface is decorated with skulls. The skull was a symbol for fame, glory, or defeat, depending on the situation. The stone below is one kind of stone that was used for the act of sacrifice. The victim would have been stretched over this stone while having his heart plucked out.

The skull symbol often appears in Aztec art

MOUNTAINTOP SACRIFICE
This ornate Moche water pot depicts men sitting high up in the mountain peaks. Mountaintops were sacred places. Here people worshiped the earth gods, who were the providers of water and agriculture, and made human sacrifices to them. Water was considered to be the blood of agricultural life. Human sacrifices were performed for many reasons. They were generally considered a present to the gods in exchange for a favor requested – such as a good harvest. Those who were sacrificed were thought to be fortunate, since they were guaranteed a life of ease in the world to come.

High mountains and volcanoes were important places for sacred rituals

FLAYED ALIVE
This 19th-century illustration shows human sacrifice by flaying, or skinning a man alive. The ancient Peruvians performed this kind of ritual sacrifice. Skinning was also practiced by the ancient Mexicans during agricultural festivities. Like the ancient Mexicans, the ancient Peruvians had many sacrificial victims dedicated to the sun Inti or to the creator god Viracocha.

Medicine

IN MESOAMERICA and in the Andean cultures, treatments for illnesses were based on a mixture of magic and a certain knowledge of the body. Mesoamerican midwives, healers, and physicians were often women who were well versed in the use of herbs. The Andeans believed that disease had a supernatural cause. They treated the sick with herbs for both magical and medicinal reasons. The Aztecs used certain minerals for medicine, as well as the flesh of some animals. The Incas used urine for treating fever, and often bled themselves. Inca surgeons bored holes in the skull and amputated limbs when necessary. Both Mesoamericans and Andeans used obsidian knives and lancets for surgery.

Bather resting in steam bath

Taking a steam bath was part of the treatment to cure the sick in Mesoamerica.

Snakeroot, taken for stomach pains

Pudding pipe-tree, a laxative, good for coughs and fever

MEDICINE SELECTION
Various plants and herbs were used as medicine. This root (left) was taken for rheumatism, and to treat bites of poisonous animals. Some roots were particularly useful for treating kidney complaints, and round beans (below) were taken for circulation ailments. Quinine (from the bark of a Peruvian tree), despite its bitter taste, was taken to prevent and treat malaria.

Rabbit fern, good for treating rheumatism

Palm nuts, good for circulation

Quinine, taken for malaria

BANDAGING A LEG
Physicians had a good knowledge of the body, and they were often right in their diagnoses. This Aztec surgeon is bandaging an injured leg.

MAN SUFFERING FROM TUBERCULOSIS
Like the Andeans, the Aztecs portrayed diseases and deformities in their art. This sculpture is of a man suffering from tuberculosis, one of the most serious ailments in ancient Mexico. Tuberculosis afflicted many young people. The realism of the sculpture allows us to see the deformed back caused by the disease.

POT SHOWING MAN WITH SPOTS
Although the Spanish conquistadors brought many unknown diseases into South America, the Andeans seem to have known some serious diseases before their arrival. Examples of some diseases were *uta* (a kind of leprosy) and syphilis. The man portrayed on this Chancay vessel may have suffered from either disease.

Peyote

MARKET MEDICINE STALL

In Mesoamerica, wild plants and herbs were cultivated in botanical gardens for medicinal purposes and sold in markets. There were roots, seeds, maguey leaves, *copal* resin, and all kinds of plants for treating a range of ailments from snake bites to gout and fever. The ancient Mexicans believed that *copal* smoke cured diseases. Tobacco powder was inhaled by the Andeans to help clear the head, but in Mesoamerica it was also smoked for pleasure. Many seeds and roots were combined with vanilla, cocoa, and maize to make the medicine more palatable although many of these flavorings were considered medicinal in their own right.

CACTUS TOPS

Some plants and seeds, such as *ololiuhqui* seeds (morning glory), were taken by the ancient Mexicans for medicinal purposes. These seeds as well as *peyote* (above), or cactus tops, from northern Mexico were widely taken as drugs. People who ate them experienced colorful hallucinations. Drugs causing hallucinations were also consumed in order for people to communicate with the gods.

Snakeskins and snake flesh were taken for various illnesses

Nuts and seeds

Leaves and roots

Writing and counting

BOTH THE MESOAMERICAN people and the ancient Peruvians kept records. However, what they recorded and how they did this was very different. Mesoamerican cultures had a picture-writing system and kept details of their history and administration; the Peruvians had no written records. The Incas recorded information about tribute (p. 27) and goods in storage upon the *quipu*, an arrangement of knotted strings. Many Mesoamerican pictures (or glyphs) were pictograms, where an object was represented by a drawing. These glyphs also described ideas; for example, a shield and a club signified war. This kind of writing has been kept in books (called codices), painted on walls and vases, and carved into objects ranging from stone monuments to tiny pieces of jade. The Mesoamericans were obsessed by counting and the passage of time. Both the Aztecs and the Maya devised a *vigesimal* counting system, based on the unit 20, and had two calendars, the solar calendar and the sacred almanac.

ANCIENT AZTEC GODS
According to Aztec mythology the most ancient gods and the creators of the universe were "Lord and Lady of our sustenance." They are associated with time and the calendar.

Quipus were used to record the census and for taxation purposes

INCA COUNTING DEVICE
The *quipu* was a length of cord held horizontally, from which knotted strings of various thicknesses and colors hung vertically. The information recorded varied according to the types of knots, the length of the cord, and the color and position of the strings.

Numbers recorded with knots of varying sizes

HIGH SOCIETY
Only the elite, a small fraction of Mesoamerican society, could read and interpret written records. This Maya woman is reading a book on her knee.

AZTEC DAYS OF THE MONTH
The Aztec solar calendar year was 365 days long. It consisted of 18 months of 20 days and five extra days that were thought to be unlucky. This illustration shows four days of the month – flint knife, rain, flower, and alligator.

MAYA PAINTED BOOK
There are four Maya codices in existence. This one, the Codex Tro-Cortesianus, contains information about divination (predicting the future) and rituals for Maya priests. Codices were made of carefully prepared paper, cloth made from fibers of the maguey plant, or animal skin. The Maya codices were written or painted with fine brushes on long strips of bark paper, folded like screens and covered with a layer of chalky paste (gesso).

INCA ACCOUNTANT
A special accountant was in charge of keeping records. He was skilled in recording figures, whether of people, llamas, or what tribute was to be paid.

Facsimile copy of original Codex Tro-Cortesianus

Sun, or lord of the earth

One of the previous four world creations

This band shows the 20 days of the month

AZTEC SUN STONE
This stone is the largest Aztec sculpture ever found, measuring 13.2 ft (4 m) in diameter. At the center of the stone is the face of the sun, or that of the lord of the earth. This carving is sometimes called the "Calendar Stone." In fact, it represents the Aztec belief that the universe had passed through four world creations, which had been destroyed. We are now in the fifth, doomed to be destroyed by earthquakes. According to Aztec mythology, the sun, the moon, and human beings were successfully created at the beginning of the fifth era.

The date glyph on this sculpture is "day one death"

RIDDLE OF THE GLYPHS
The study of Maya hieroglyphic writing started in 1827. By 1950, names of gods and animals had been identified. In 1960, researchers realized that Maya inscriptions were primarily historical. They deal with the births, accessions, wars, deaths, and marriages of Maya kings. This Maya stone carving was placed over doors and windows. It has a glyph that dates it to the sixth century.

BUNDLE OF YEARS
The Aztecs divided time into "centuries" of 52 years. At the end of each cycle and the beginning of a new one an Aztec ceremony called "the binding of the years" took place. In sculpture each cycle is represented by a bundle of "reeds" accompanied by dates. This sculpted stone bundle symbolizes the death of an Aztec century.

Bars and dots are Mayan glyphs for numbers

This codex was read from top to bottom, and from left to right

Glyphs showing five gods

Glyphs painted onto fine layer of gesso

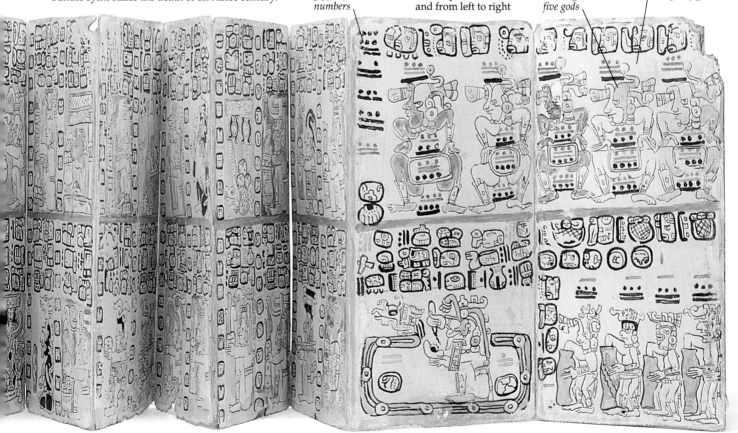

Weaving and spinning

Much of the sophisticated Andean weaving was made on the back-strap loom

NO OTHER PEOPLE in the Americas have left such a wealth of marvelous woven textiles as the ancient Peruvians have. Their exquisitely worked textiles have survived in graves in areas of Peru that have a desert-like climate. The tradition of weaving and spinning was practiced by all women, both in Mesoamerica and in the Andean region. Women were expected to spin and weave for their families' needs, and to contribute woven goods as payment of tribute and taxes to the rulers. Textiles were woven mainly from cotton and maguey fiber in Mesoamerica, while alpaca and llama wool were widely used in the Andean region.

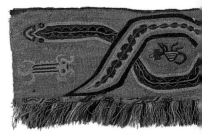

Nazca textile with fringed border

Loom bar, attached to a tree or post

Long threads fixed to the loom bars are called the warp

NATURAL DYES
In Mesoamerica, cotton was used for making textiles for the upper classes; maguey, yucca, and palm fibers were woven for the commoners. The yarn was dyed before it was woven. Some dyes were made from the juice of flowers and fruits, but dyes were also extracted from shellfish and from the cochineal, a tiny insect that lives on the cactus plant.

Shed rod

BACK-STRAP LOOM
The most common loom used throughout the Americas was the back-strap loom (left). It is still widely used today. The loom consists of two loom bars, poles holding the warp, which are hooked to a support at one end, and pulled taut by a belt around the weaver's back at the other end. The weft (horizontal) thread is passed under and over the strands of the warp (vertical) threads using a heddle stick and a shed rod to lift up alternate strands. To alter the pattern or introduce more color, more heddles are used, or different groups of warp threads are lifted up.

Heddle stick grasped with left hand

Weft threads run alternately under and over warp threads

Weaving sword used to smooth down weft threads

Figurine may be of Mayan goddess Ixchel, patroness of weaving

Strap fitted around weaver's waist

MAYA LADY WEAVING
This Maya figurine shows a young lady sitting on the ground, weaving with a back-strap loom.

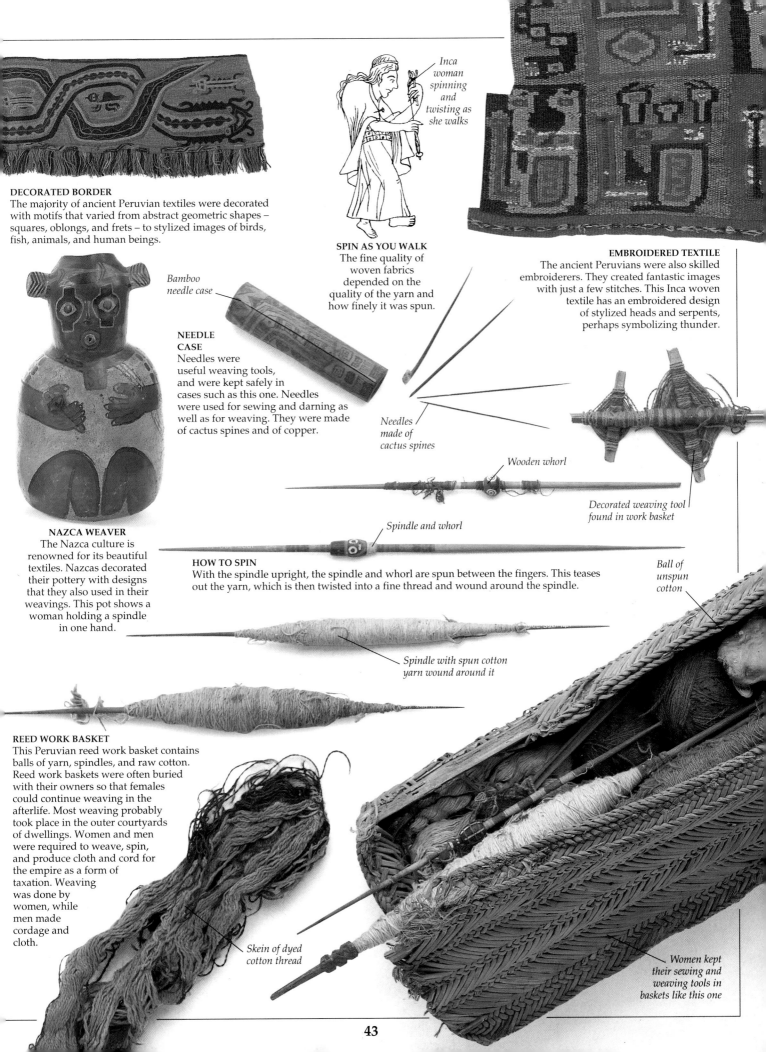

DECORATED BORDER
The majority of ancient Peruvian textiles were decorated with motifs that varied from abstract geometric shapes – squares, oblongs, and frets – to stylized images of birds, fish, animals, and human beings.

Inca woman spinning and twisting as she walks

SPIN AS YOU WALK
The fine quality of woven fabrics depended on the quality of the yarn and how finely it was spun.

EMBROIDERED TEXTILE
The ancient Peruvians were also skilled embroiderers. They created fantastic images with just a few stitches. This Inca woven textile has an embroidered design of stylized heads and serpents, perhaps symbolizing thunder.

Bamboo needle case

NEEDLE CASE
Needles were useful weaving tools, and were kept safely in cases such as this one. Needles were used for sewing and darning as well as for weaving. They were made of cactus spines and of copper.

Needles made of cactus spines

Wooden whorl

Decorated weaving tool found in work basket

Spindle and whorl

NAZCA WEAVER
The Nazca culture is renowned for its beautiful textiles. Nazcas decorated their pottery with designs that they also used in their weavings. This pot shows a woman holding a spindle in one hand.

HOW TO SPIN
With the spindle upright, the spindle and whorl are spun between the fingers. This teases out the yarn, which is then twisted into a fine thread and wound around the spindle.

Ball of unspun cotton

Spindle with spun cotton yarn wound around it

REED WORK BASKET
This Peruvian reed work basket contains balls of yarn, spindles, and raw cotton. Reed work baskets were often buried with their owners so that females could continue weaving in the afterlife. Most weaving probably took place in the outer courtyards of dwellings. Women and men were required to weave, spin, and produce cloth and cord for the empire as a form of taxation. Weaving was done by women, while men made cordage and cloth.

Skein of dyed cotton thread

Women kept their sewing and weaving tools in baskets like this one

Clothes and accessories

CLOTHING styles were very different in Mesoamerica and South America, but in both regions they reflected a person's social class. People who wore clothes of fine material with colorful and elaborate decoration were of high status. The Incas made their clothes from wool, although on the coast cotton was preferred. Alpaca wool was worn by ordinary people and silky vicuna wool by the nobles. In Mesoamerica, garments were made from cotton or other plant fibers. All items of clothing were very simple. Many were just a piece of material draped around a part of the body. Men from both regions wore loincloths. Aztec women wore a skirt wrapped around the hips. Men wore cloaks draped over the shoulder. Some items of clothing – ponchos and tunics – slipped over the head and were sewn at the sides.

CAPPING IT ALL
In the Andean region people wore knitted wool or cotton caps. This handsome Chimu cap with colorful panels is unusual because it is made from woven wool.

SANDAL
The Incas made sandals with leather from the neck of the llama. In other regions sandals were made of wool or, as in this case, the fiber of the aloe plant.

Braided wool fastening

IN THE BAG
All Peruvian men carried a small bag under their cloak, slung over the shoulder. In it they carried coca leaves for chewing, and amulets (good-luck charms).

SLEEVELESS PONCHO *right*
Some ponchos were decorated with fine patterns. They were such important garments that the dead were buried with ponchos. In the highland regions of Peru, both men and women wear ponchos to the present day.

Woven headband

ANDEAN WOMAN'S DRESS
Although this is an 18th-century impression of a Peruvian woman, her clothing is similar to that worn by an Inca woman: a long dress of woven rectangular cloth, with a long cloak and sandals.

CHILD'S PONCHO *left*
Finely woven ponchos covering mummies have been discovered in some ancient Peruvian graves. This small poncho was discovered in a child's grave. It is woven from wool, with a design of birds in diagonal bands.

SHELL NECKLACE
In Mesoamerica, only the ruler and nobles could wear jewelry such as headbands, armbands, or nose, lip, and earplugs. Even necklaces made of shells like this one could not be worn by everyone.

DIFFERENT CLOTHES, DIFFERENT JOBS
Aztec people wore clothes that suited their role in society. The lavish headdresses and rich materials worn here show that these are people of high rank.

COORDINATED CLOTHES
This Mayan woman is wearing a matching turban, skirt, and shawl. Her beautiful long hair is tied back with white ribbons. She wears a feather ornament in one ear and a bracelet probably made of leather.

Parasol

Elaborate headdress with two folds

SOPHISTICATED LADY
This richly attired figure is obviously a high-ranking Mayan woman. She wears a headdress with two folds, and blue earplugs that perhaps represent turquoise. Her beaded necklace, is similar in shape to Mayan jade necklaces and she wears bracelets on both arms. With one hand she protects her face with a parasol.

FANCY CAPE
Capes like this one were worn throughout Mesoamerica. This army commander is of high rank, so his cape is finely decorated.

Robe with holes for arms and square-cut neck

MALE FASHION
This life-size head of a Mixtec man shows what adornments they wore. He has a headband tied around his forehead, with a bird's head at the center, and blue disks at the sides. His hair is loose, and he wears round blue earplugs. His mouth is painted with black and white spots, resembling a mouth ornament.

Mayan women often walked barefoot

Master potters

MAYAN FRESCO VASE
This cylindrical pot, decorated with the figure of a jaguar, was a common shape among the Mayas. It was covered with stucco and then painted over while still wet.

THE DECORATED CERAMICS of ancient Andean cultures are one of their most striking achievements. The Mesoamericans also had a rich and varied pottery tradition. Potters did not use a potter's wheel in either region. They produced a wide range of shapes, which they painted, carved, or stamped for decoration. The finest ceramics were for the rich or for ritual use. Pottery for everyday use was more simple. Because the Andean cultures had no writing system, pottery is a valuable source of information about the societies that made it, and their religious ideas and cultural influences.

ARYBALLOS JAR
Inca pottery is of excellent quality, and is made in a few standard shapes. The most typical is the "aryballos" jar, with a conical base and tall, flaring neck.

Jar used for storing water or possibly chicha beer

MOCHE FROG VESSEL
Moche potters based their designs on fanciful and realistic images, and modeled many animals, human figures, and plants. Pots with stirrup spouts, such as this one, often served as "libation" vessels, used for making liquid offerings to the gods.

Nazca vessel unrolled to show decoration

NAZCA POT
The Nazca civilization is distinctive for its pottery, decorated in many colors with both realistic and mythological creatures, such as this demon with a human body.

Stirrup-spout vessel in the shape of a frog

Jade and shell eyes   *Pieces of shell*

CHICKEN VESSEL
This is a good example of the creativity and imagination of the potters from Teotihuacán. The eyes of this "chicken" are made of jade and shell, and the body is decorated with conch shells.

How a pot was made, its shape, and the motifs decorating it help researchers discover when it was made

PAINTING PALETTE
It is very likely that the Teotihuacán potters used some kind of palette to mix pigments. They used both vegetable and mineral colors. This pottery object may have been used as a palette for the pigments.

FIGURINE AND MOLD
This figurine of a goddess with two children was modeled using a clay mold. It may have been placed on the altar in a peasant house, as peasants could not afford anything bigger or of better material.

Clay goddess   Mold for goddess

Aztec potters usually decorated the inside of bowls

AZTEC BOWL
The decoration on this bowl is based on an abstract pattern of zigzag lines. Painted decoration was usually only in two colors, as on this bowl.

Hummingbird perched on rim

This urn contained human ashes

MIXTEC CUP
This beautiful Mixtec cup is decorated with a hummingbird perched on the rim. The base has the characteristic "step fret" motif often used by Mixtec artists.

"Step fret" motif

Urn found at the Great Temple of the Aztecs

FUNERARY URN
Some clay vessels were not painted, but rather the decoration was cut into the surface. The picture on one side of this urn is of a bearded god wearing a necklace. He holds a spearthrower in one hand, and spears in the other.

Featherwork

THE BRIGHT COLORS and natural sheen of tropical bird feathers made them a valuable item for trade and tribute in Mesoamerica and in the Andean region of South America. Tropical birds were hunted and raised in captivity for their feathers, which were worked into stunning patterns and designs. For the Mesoamericans, the iridescent green feathers of the quetzal were the most prized. The Incas used feathers as part of their dress and wove them into clothing for special occasions. They also used them to decorate headdresses and tunics, and to make mosaics (a design of feathers glued to a backing to decorate hard items such as shields). Skilled Aztec featherworkers made beautiful garments only for the nobility, while the Mayas made superb items such as headdresses that were extended at the back and made the wearer look like a bird that had just landed.

FEATHER MOSAICS
Ancient Mexico had a guild of expert featherworkers who used intricate methods of gluing and weaving feather mosaics. These methods were studied and illustrated by a Spanish friar called Bernardino de Sahagún.

Tall feather headdress

FEATHER SHIRT AND HEADDRESS
This type of feather shirt is known as a *poncho*. Each of the feathers has been carefully stitched to a cotton cloth to make up the design of stylized owls and fish. Several Peruvian cultures, such as the Chimu and the Inca, had expert featherworkers.

Fan made of macaw feathers

Holder made of braided brown wool

WAVE OF COLOR
The ancient Peruvians made very colorful fans using feathers from tropical birds. These fans were useful for keeping cool in hot climates. The Peruvians made many practical objects with feathers, especially from parrots and macaws, as these were their favorite birds.

Strings were used
to tie the headdress
around the head

FEATHER HEADDRESS
This simple Peruvian headdress was made from feathers
possibly taken from birds in the Amazon region. Items made
from the feathers of exotic birds were status symbols.

MONTEZUMA'S HEADDRESS
This is a replica of a headdress said to have
belonged to Montezuma, the last Aztec
ruler. The headdress was part of the booty
sent by Cortés to Spain (pp. 62–63). It is
made of green quetzal feathers,
blue cotinga feathers,
and gold
disks.

*Headdress
contains the
feathers of at
least 250 birds*

*Fan has a
butterfly on
this side and
a flower on
the other*

*Feather
headdress*

MEXICAN FAN
This fan was
made with the
feathers of several
kinds of bird.
Sumptuous fans such as this
one were used by dignitaries.

Bamboo handle

loak of
ellow and
reen feathers

Rear
view

Front
view

Side
view

WARRIOR OUTFIT
An Aztec warrior's
rank was reflected
in the kind of
feather suit he
wore. This
elaborate
feather suit,
complete with
shield and
headdress, was
worn by a
high-ranking
warrior.

*Feather
headdress*

Feather suit
belonging to
a warrior of
high status

*Feather
shield*

FEATHERS IN STONE
This carved stone Atlantean figure
from a temple at Chichén Itzá was
originally painted all over. The
watercolors show two views of it
as it would have been. The figure
is dressed in a full-length feather
cloak and a feather headdress.

REBUILDING THE PAST
Watercolors like this one
by British artist Adela
Breton give us an idea of how
pre-Columbian sculptures were
painted, and what the buildings
at Chichén Itzá looked
like originally.

*Feather
suit*

Precious metals

LIP ORNAMENT
Eagle heads like this one made by the Mixtecs were popular as decoration for lip plugs, or labrets. The Mixtecs produced most of the gold work for the Aztec elite. Labrets were inserted through a hole made below the bottom lip.

THE PERUVIAN TRADITION of crafting magnificent artifacts from precious metals began 3,500 years ago, the age of the oldest piece of precious metalwork found in the Andes. Methods of metalworking gradually developed, and metals were widely worked in South America before the Christian era. They were introduced to Mesoamerica about 850 B.C. Some of the most common precious metals in the Americas are gold, silver, and platinum. These were mostly used for making objects for ritual use, trinkets, and jewelry. Combinations of gold and silver, and gold and copper (called *tumbaga*), were also used. Because of the value attached to gold, wearing gold jewelry was a sign of a person's wealth and power. When a wealthy person died, his or her tomb would be filled with precious gold and silver objects, encrusted with precious stones.

GOLD CREATURE
The ancient South American goldsmiths produced many and fantastic creatures. This figure is a mixture of human and animal forms.

PORTRAIT CUP
This cup is called a "portrait cup," as it seems to portray the face of a real person. Portrait cups were often made of pounded silver.

Almond-shaped eyes

Aquiline nose

Cup has hammered bird design

SILVER DRINKING CUP
These cups are usually known as *keros*. Many of them have been found throughout the Andean region, placed in cemeteries together with other objects near the corpses. Some *keros* were used to drink *chicha*, a kind of beer made of maize. Some cups were inlaid with turquoise. This cup is the work of a Chimu metalsmith, showing it was made before the Inca period.

ELEGANT NECKLACE
Of the few gold objects that have survived from the Basin of Mexico, most have been found at the Great Temple of the Aztecs. The beads of this necklace were made of hollow gold. Some of them are plain, and others are decorated with a spiral design.

GOLD IN THE NOSE
This Mixtec ornament is one of the few nose plugs that have survived. Some nose ornaments are in the shape of butterflies and other creatures. The beauty of this one lies in its simplicity.

Thunderbolt

BAT RATTLE
This cast gold rattle represents a bat god. The god is holding a thunderbolt in one hand and a throwing stick in the other.

PANNING FOR GOLD
Most of the gold used by the Peruvian Indians was obtained from "placer" mines in rivers, where the gold is near the surface. They used fire-hardened digging sticks to break up the earth, and shallow trays in which to carry and wash it.

Charcoal-heated furnace, kept hot by blowing through a tube

Figure holds a standard or banner

Hooked earrings

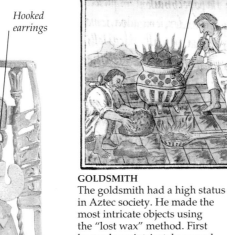

GOLDSMITH
The goldsmith had a high status in Aztec society. He made the most intricate objects using the "lost wax" method. First he made an intricately carved beeswax mold, and carefully covered it with a layer of clay. When it was heated, melted wax flowed out and the mold was filled with molten metal. In this illustration, the goldsmith is about to pour molten gold into a mold.

LIME SCOOPS
These tiny lime scoops were used in the preparation of a drug called *coca*. Powdered lime was scooped onto a coca leaf, made into a ball, and chewed.

Handle has figure of a hummingbird

Handle has figure of a monkey

Llamas were highly valued in the Andean region. Many stylized llama figurines were made

ZAPOTEC GOLD FIGURE
Many gold items seem to depict important people or gods. The items they wear and hold may have had a symbolic meaning for the Mesoamerican people, but we can only guess what it symbolizes. This standing gold figure was probably the work of a Zapotec goldsmith. The figure is wearing a pendant around its neck. Three bells hang from the pendant's head.

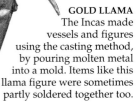

GOLD LLAMA
The Incas made vessels and figures using the casting method, by pouring molten metal into a mold. Items like this llama figure were sometimes partly soldered together too.

Precious stones

THE INCAS, MAYAS, AND AZTECS had a taste for all kinds of stones, and their skilled craftsmen fashioned exquisite objects from them. The Incas favored turquoise, which they used as inlay in gold and silver objects. The Mesoamericans favored stones of different colors with shiny surfaces, such as jade and green stones in general, turquoise, onyx, rock crystal, and porphyry (a dark red rock), among others. They made jewelry and a variety of containers, masks, and sculptures. Jade was the most precious material, according to the Mesoamerican people. It was associated with water, the life-giving fluid, and with the color of the maize plant, their staple food. Turquoise was also highly valued and was laboriously worked both in Mesoamerica and in the Andean regions.

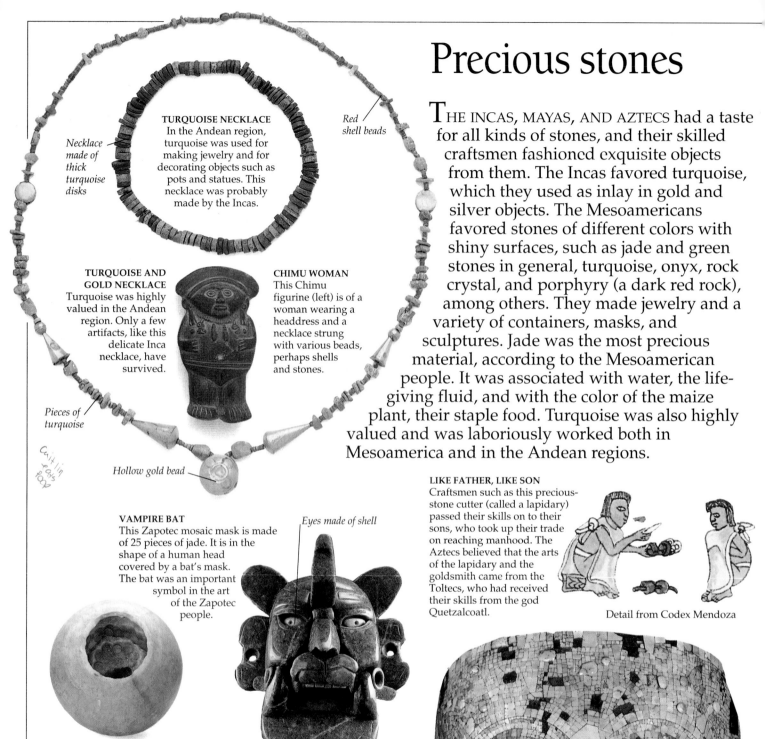

TURQUOISE NECKLACE
In the Andean region, turquoise was used for making jewelry and for decorating objects such as pots and statues. This necklace was probably made by the Incas.

Necklace made of thick turquoise disks

Red shell beads

TURQUOISE AND GOLD NECKLACE
Turquoise was highly valued in the Andean region. Only a few artifacts, like this delicate Inca necklace, have survived.

CHIMU WOMAN
This Chimu figurine (left) is of a woman wearing a headdress and a necklace strung with various beads, perhaps shells and stones.

Pieces of turquoise

Hollow gold bead

LIKE FATHER, LIKE SON
Craftsmen such as this precious-stone cutter (called a lapidary) passed their skills on to their sons, who took up their trade on reaching manhood. The Aztecs believed that the arts of the lapidary and the goldsmith came from the Toltecs, who had received their skills from the god Quetzalcoatl.

Detail from Codex Mendoza

VAMPIRE BAT
This Zapotec mosaic mask is made of 25 pieces of jade. It is in the shape of a human head covered by a bat's mask. The bat was an important symbol in the art of the Zapotec people.

Eyes made of shell

ONYX CUP
In Mesoamerica, onyx was used for making objects for the elite. The craftsman would begin with a large lump of onyx, cutting out the center with obsidian tools (above). Many onyx objects are rounded, like this cup (below), as this was the easiest shape to produce.

Eyes and teeth made of shell

TURQUOISE MASK *right*
One of the most remarkable Mesoamerican arts was that of mosaic making, especially using turquoise. This mask, representing the god Quetzalcoatl, is one of the best preserved examples of Mexican turquoise mosaic.

MASK OF A KING
When the Mayan lord Pacal died, he was buried below a magnificent temple pyramid at Palenque. His corpse was covered with jewels and objects made from precious stones, such as jade. This jade mosaic mask, with eyes of inlaid shell and obsidian, covered his face. Each of his fingers was adorned with jade rings.

Warrior's face peering out of coyote mask

COYOTE WARRIOR
This Toltec ornament is a unique example of Toltec craftsmanship. It is also unique for what it represents – a coyote warrior from the Toltec city of Tula. The head is covered with mother-of-pearl mosaic.

FANCY TATTOOS
As well as wearing jewelry, Mesoamericans tattooed their bodies. This was a widespread practice in the whole of Mesoamerica.

This piece rested behind the lip, against the gum

JADE LABRET
The Mesoamerican labret (lip plug) was an ornament that was worn below the lower lip. The Aztecs made labrets for the members of the elite out of many materials, especially gold and jade.

JADE NECKLACE
This Olmec necklace with a human head was worn by a member of the elite. The wealthy in Mesoamerica wore many body adornments, such as necklaces and bracelets.

Coyote with jaws wide open

Green stones were valued more than any other material in Mesoamerica

Masks

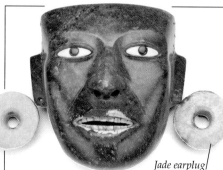

FOR HUNDREDS OF YEARS, masks fashioned from materials such as gold, obsidian, jade, and wood – some inlaid with turquoise and coral – have been worn in the Americas. Masks were commonly placed over mummy bundles to protect the deceased from the dangers of the afterlife. They were also worn for festivals. Among the Incas and the Aztecs, for whom music and dance (pp. 56–57) were a form of religious expression, masks and costumes had a symbolic meaning. Even today in Mesoamerica and in the Andean region, people still wear masks during festivals.

Jade earplug

HUMAN MASK
This finely carved greenstone mask, found at the Great Temple of the Aztecs, was an offering to the gods. It is inlaid with shell and obsidian, and its earlobes are pierced to attach earplugs.

HAMMERED COPPER MASK
Masks such as this copper one (left) have been found on mummies in many Andean burial sites. The wealthier the individual the more elaborate was their burial and the more expensive the fabrics that wrapped and decorated the mummy bundle.

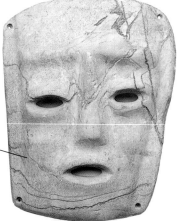

Mask made of stone

Holes in mask may have had hair threaded through them

FACE VALUE
Many objects from the Mezcala region, including masks, were found at the Great Temple of the Aztecs. This mask was paid as tribute to the Aztecs (pp. 26–27).

MAYAN HEAD
Many heads and masks give an idea of what people looked like. This head shows that the Mayas practiced cranial deformation, which means that they forced the top of the head to grow taller and slope backward.

JEWELED MASK
This Chimu funerary mask is made of thin sheet gold. It would have been placed over a mummy's face. The nose ornament, decorated with gold disks, was made separately.

Eyes decorated with emerald beads

MASK FROM ANCON
Masks of all shapes, colors, and sizes have been found in Peruvian burial sites. This one was found covering a mummy's face in an enormous cemetery at Ancón, on the central coast of Peru.

Eyes made of shell

Real hair attached to mask

Turquoise mosaic pieces

TEOTIHUACAN MASK
Teotihuacán is famous for its expert mask makers, who made realistic masks from a variety of materials. This mask has mosaic pieces of turquoise and coral around the noseplug. The pupils of the eyes are made of obsidian and the whites are shell inlays.

Necklace made from coral beads

Cloth hat with real hair

HALF FELINE–HALF HUMAN MASK
Olmec art drew its inspiration from mythology and religion. One of the Olmecs' beliefs was that a woman was united with a jaguar, producing a race with features of both, as can be seen in this jade mask.

Snarling catlike face

REMARKABLE OFFERING
The Chancay tombs of southern Peru contained seated figures dressed in remarkable textiles and wooden masks. Many of these were buried with the deceased as offerings to the gods.

55

Music and dance

MUSIC, SONG, AND DANCE were an important part of Mesoamerican and South American life. Scenes of people playing music and dancing decorate many clay vases, especially those produced by Moche potters. The most common instruments in both Mesoamerica and South America were rattles, whistles, trumpets, flutes, copper bells, and shells. String instruments were practically unknown in the Americas. The music in South America was not very varied, and often musical instruments played only one tone. For these civilizations, music and dance were closely linked to religion. Everyone, from rulers to peasants, took part in dances performed especially for their gods.

MOCHE FLUTIST
Many Moche vases are realistic portraits of people and their pastimes. This one shows that flutes were played in the Andean region.

End of rattle in shape of a dog's head

CLAY TRUMPET
Moche trumpets came in straight and coiled shapes. This one ends in two catlike heads, which may represent a god. This shape of coil is typical of Moche trumpets.

Catlike heads have gaping, snarling jaws with bared fangs

In Aztec times two types of drum were played – the *huehuetl* or *tlapanhuehuetl* (vertical drum) and the *teponaztli*, or horizontal drum

Pole decorated with paper sheets and flags

FEAST FOR THE DEAD
Dance and music were an important part of feasts and ritual occasions. This illustration shows men holding hands, dancing around a pole, at a feast for the dead. The pole is festooned with paper sheets and three big flags, one of which has a feather decoration. The Aztecs adorned an image of the dead person with flags. This feast lasted all day, and people danced to the beat of the drum, played by a priest. The dancers in this illustration were captives who were later burned as sacrifice.

Drum covered with a feline's pelt

INCA PANPIPES
The most commonly played Andean musical instrument was the syrinx, or panpipes. They were usually made from cane or clay. The delicate sounds are produced by blowing across one end of the panpipes. These Inca panpipes are made from the quills of a bird of prey called the condor.

Quills held together by a horizontal quill, tied with string

Panpipes are made of tubes of different lengths

MUSICAL CELEBRATIONS
Most Inca instruments were wind and percussion instruments. In this fiesta the women are singing, dancing, and playing the drum, while the men are playing flutes, or *quenas*.

CLAY RATTLE
Rattles were made of clay, metal, or strings of large seeds. This Moche rattle has a dog's head at one end. The handle of the rattle is in the shape of a man's head.

Man's head

UNIQUE FLUTE
The Mesoamerican people played all kinds of flutes, from simple straight ones to more complex ones such as this, decorated with a figure of a woman standing on a disk that has several openings. This type of flute is unique to Mesoamerica. It was probably played in religious ceremonies.

BEATING THE RHYTHM
The horizontal drum, the *teponaztli*, was a hollowed log with a hole in the bottom and slotted at the top; it was played with drumsticks with rubber tips. This codex illustration (right) shows an Aztec orchestra with a similar drum. The decoration of drums varied from intricate carvings to realistic animal or human forms. Some drums were painted or gilded. The carving on this drum is of a person with loose hair, wearing a tasseled headdress decorated with feathers.

AZTEC ORCHESTRA
Gourd (or gourd-shaped) rattles were an essential part of dance. They are depicted in Aztec books and in Maya mural paintings. This illustration shows men shaking rattles and two drummers, one playing the *teponaztli* and the other the *huehuetl*.

57

Sports and games

GAME OF THE CENTURY
The game *patolli* was played on a board with four divisions. Beans were used as dice, and the "checkers" were little stones of different colors. The board had 52 parts, like the Aztec ritual cycle of 52 years.

EVERY ASPECT of Aztec life, including sports and games revolved around religion. The two main games played by the Aztecs were *patolli*, a board game similar to backgammon, and the ball game *ulama*. *Ulama* was played in Mesoamerica long before the Aztecs by other ancient Mexican civilizations, such as the Mayas. As well as being a sport, the ball game had a religious meaning. The ball court represented the world, and the ball stood for the moon and the sun. Bets were placed on the outcome of the game, and some players lost everything they had – including their lives.

THE WRESTLER
This basalt sculpture of an athlete with raised arms and an arched back suggests that the Olmec people may have practiced some form of wrestling.

Arm protector

Only nobles could play the ball game

Padded hip protector

Ball players propelled the ball with the hips

BALL COURT RING
Players had to propel the ball through rings such as this one in order to score points. The rings had various decorations on them, such as snakes and monkeys. When the Spaniards arrived in Mexico (pp. 62–63), they found many stone rings jutting out from the walls of ball courts.

BALL PLAYER IN ACTION
Mayan figurines showing ball players in action give an excellent idea of the many elements of the ball game costume. Players wore helmets as well as gloves and padded knee and hip protectors made of hide. All of these were essential protection against the solid rubber ball.

STONE AX

Axes, or *hachas* (above), were used by several Mesoamerican cultures as part of the ball game. They may have been worn attached to the front of the yoke in ritual processions.

Ax in the shape of a human head

Elaborately carved greenstone yoke

BALL COURT

This ball court at Chichén Itzá is shaped like a capital I. To aim the ball through the rings was extremely difficult, as the rings were set 27 ft (8 m) high.

PLAYING BALL

No one knows exactly how the ball game was played, but we do know that it was played by two teams, each with two or three players, using a solid rubber ball in specially made courts. The game was dangerous because of the speed at which the ball was propelled from one side of the court to the other, using the hips – using hands and feet was not allowed. The game varied according to when and where it was played.

GREENSTONE YOKE

Yugos or stone yokes (left), and axes (above left) such as these are probably replicas of wooden or leather paraphernalia used in the ceremonial ball game. Large, horseshoe-shaped yokes were worn around the waist of the player as protective belts. Stone yokes were probably used as molds for making copies in leather or wood.

BALL MARKER

Stone markers, such as this one which is about 7 ft (2 m) tall, were placed on each side of the ball court. In Mayan courts there were as many as three markers set into the floor. It is not clear how the game was scored, or exactly what the markers were used for.

Blood in the form of snakes

SYMBOLIC GAME

There were many beliefs surrounding the ball game. The game's violent competition was a symbol of the battle between darkness (night) and light (day), and was a reenactment of the death and rebirth of the sun. People also believed that the more they played the ball game, the better their harvest would be.

Ball court ring

Codex illustration of a ball court

LOSER LOSES ALL

The stakes were high for the opposing teams in a ballgame. The losing team was often sacrificed. This sculpted panel shows a decapitated ballplayer. The blood streaming from his neck is pictured as snakes, which were symbols of agricultural fertility.

Bestiary

ANIMAL LIFE in the Americas was very rich and varied. Animals played an important part in everyday life as well as in the religions of both regions. Many works of art are decorated with images of animals that had religious significance - foxes, owls, jaguars, hummingbirds, eagles, and llamas. Some animals were domesticated - the turkey and dog in Mesoamerica, and the llama and the alpaca in the Andean region. With their relatives, guanacos and vicuñas, llamas and alpacas were valued for their wool, meat and as beasts of burden. In both regions, deer, rabbits, ducks, and many other kinds of edible birds, abounded. Animal life in the tropical forests included the largest cat in the world, the jaguar, which was worshiped and feared, along with snakes.

BIRD ASSORTMENT
Mesoamerica had a variety of brilliantly coloured tropical birds such as parrots, macaws, and quetzals. Their feathers were used to decorate many objects and clothes (pp. 48–49).

QUETZAL BIRD
This bird was greatly valued by the ancient Mesoamericans, for whom its long, deep green feathers were as precious as jade or gold. Some of their gods were covered in quetzal feathers, and they were also used to make the headdresses of rulers and kings.

This Toltec vessel is an example of plumbate pottery – lead in the clay gives the pot a metallic finish

BIRD TAPESTRY *above*
The Paracas culture is renowned for the abundant, ornate textiles that were placed alongside the dead. This textile fragment is decorated with a typical Paracas design of stylized birds.

Figure has catlike claws and ears and a monkey's tail

FABRIC "DEVIL"
Many textiles from Paracas are woven or embroidered with animal images, often in a stylized form. Sometimes it is difficult to identify the animal in question, because of the geometric forms.

FOX
Animals such as the fox, which hunted and killed other animals, were in turn hunted by the Aztecs and the Incas. This Moche vessel is in the shape of a snarling fox.

TOLTEC CERAMIC DOG
Some breeds of dog were fattened and eaten by the Aztecs and the Mayas, but the Incas found eating dog meat a disgusting habit. The Mesoamericans used dogs as companions in hunting expeditions. According to their religion, dogs were also necessary for the journey to the afterlife, as they helped the dead cross rivers.

Stirrup-spouted Moche vessel in form of a fox's head.

Vicuñas live on the grasslands of the Andean mountains

Vicuñas reach a height of 30 in (80 cm) at the shoulder

ARMADILLO
The Aztecs ate the meat of the armadillo, which is white and tastes like chicken. Among the Mayas, the armadillo was associated with the afterlife.

Some armadillos grow to a length of 4 ft (120 cm)

The armadillo is a nocturnal mammal that lives in tropical areas

VICUNAS
Like the alpaca, the vicuña (above) was a good wool-producing animal. Vicuñas had the most elegant, silklike wool. Garments woven from vicuña wool were worn by the Inca nobility.

ALPACA
The alpaca lives in the Andean highlands. It was kept in herds by the ancient Peruvians because, along with the vicuña, its long wool was ideal for weaving. Its relatives the guanaco and the llama were killed for food, though the llama was mostly used for carrying loads. The ancient Andean people made offerings to this animal, as it was an important contribution to their livelihood.

Zapotec vessel probably used as an incense burner

Ocelot

OCELOT
This wildcat is sometimes known as the Mexican tiger. The ocelot was a greatly feared creature. Some warriors wore ocelot skins when going to battle.

Jaguars, ocelots, and pumas lived in tropical forests

PUMA
The puma is an animal native to the Americas. It was hunted for its skin.

Puma

Jaguar

SACRED JAGUAR
The jaguar was one of the most powerful symbols in Mesoamerica and South America. Its strength, ferocity, cunning, and hunting ability were greatly admired. This Zapotec vessel (far right) is in the shape of a jaguar standing on three legs.

Leg decorated with head of a baby jaguar

The Spanish conquest

WHEN THE SPANISH ARRIVED in the Americas, they knew nothing about the Andean and Mesoamerican cultures with their powerful empires, elaborate palaces, magnificent engineering works, and religions that reached into every part of their life. Neither did the inhabitants of the Americas have any knowledge of the Spanish. Many omens had forewarned Montezuma, the Aztec ruler, of an imminent disaster. The Inca ruler Huayna Capac, too, had heard that strange, bearded men had appeared on the coast. When Cortés entered Mexico in 1519 and Pizarro arrived in Peru in 1532, they easily overpowered resistance. Despite being few in number, the Spanish armies, with their horses and cannons, were stronger. Cortés had the added advantage that the Aztecs believed him to be the king and god Quetzalcoatl. Within a short time, the world of the Aztecs and the Incas was destroyed, their temples razed to the ground, and their emperors murdered. The Mayas resisted until 1542, when the Spanish established a capital at Mérida.

MONTEZUMA GREETS CORTÉS
When they first met, Cortés greeted Montezuma with a bow, and Montezuma handed him splendid presents of gold, precious stones such as jade, and feather objects. Cortés was on horseback, and Montezuma was carried in a litter. The Spanish soldiers were dressed in steel armor, while the Aztecs wore simple cotton cloaks. This meeting would prove decisive in the conquest of Mexico. Montezuma at this point was in two minds about the true nature of Cortés – was he human or god, their enemy or their savior? The events that followed proved Cortés to be the former.

MASSACRE
The conquistadors went in search of riches. If they met with resistance from the native people, the conquistadors killed them. This illustration depicts an expedition to Michoacán in the west of Mexico, where many local noblemen were killed for refusing to say where their treasures were hidden.

Warriors from the state of Tlaxcala supported the conquistadors

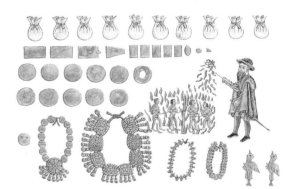

GOLDEN DEATH
This scene from Codex Kingsborough shows a Spanish tribute collector punishing the Mexican Indians at Tepetlaoztoc. A Spanish tribute collector was known as an *encomendero* (privileged Spanish colonist). The Indians being burned were late in paying their tribute. The tribute consisted of bundles of maize and gold jewelry.

Gold doubloons made from gold mined in South America

A DISEASE THAT ONLY GOLD COULD CURE
To coerce the people of Middle and South America to give them their gold, the Spanish often told them that they suffered from a disease that only gold could cure. Cortés and Pizarro both went to the Americas in search of gold and they found much of it. At the start of the conquest, Cortés sent booty to King Charles V of Spain consisting of gold and silver objects and many other goods. Over the years, huge quantities of gold were shipped to Spain. Today the ceilings of many Spanish churches are gilded with gold from the Americas.

PUNISHMENT
This illustration shows some of the punishments used by the Spanish on the Inca people, which included beating the Incas and hanging them upside down. The cruelty of many of the conquistadors made some Spanish friars devote their life to denouncing the behavior of their compatriots.

Francisco Pizarro, conquistador of Peru

GREED FOR GOLD
This caricature shows a greedy Francisco Pizarro, contemplating gold from his new Peruvian mine. Pizarro did not understand the civilization that he helped to destroy.

Wooden Inca cup made for Pizarro

CONQUISTADOR'S CUP
This wooden *kero* (p. 50) portrays the conquistador of Peru, Francisco Pizarro. Under Pizarro, Spanish control was established over the Inca empire. The Spanish forced people to abandon their irrigated lands and demanded that they mine more precious metals. Christianity was imposed upon the Incas, but they were slow to accept the new religion and continued their old practices. The Incas continued some crafts, such as weaving and making wooden *keros* like this one.

Index

Acknowledgments

Dorling Kindersley would like to thank:
Dra. Mari Carmen Serra Puche and all those who helped with photography at Museo Nacional de Antropología, Mexico City; Profesor Eduardo Matos Moctezuma and all those who helped with photography at the Great Temple Museum, Mexico City (INAH.-CNCA.-Mex); Phil Watson at the Birmingham Museum; Maureen Barry at the Royal Museum of Scotland; British Museum; Pitt Rivers Museum; Cambridge University Museum of Archaeology and Anthropology; Reynaldo Izquierdo (Mexico) and Eugene Staken for photographic assistance; Sue Giles at the City of Bristol Museum; Jabu Mahlangu, Manisha Patel, Jill Plank, and Sharon Spencer for design assistance; Katharine Thompson; Lic. Victor Hugo Vidal

Alvarez and Lic. Javier García Martínez at the Tourist Office, Mexico City; Lynn Bresler for the index; John Woodcock and Andrew Nash for illustrations.
Additional photography: Geoff Dann (24ar); Steve Gorton (39al); Peter Hayman (60cl; 60c); Dave King (61bc); James Stephenson (14bl; 62–63 top; 63bl); Jerry Young (61ar; 61cl).

Picture credits
a=above, b=below, c=center, l=left, r=right

Archaeological Museum, Lima/e.t. archive: 20bl, 38bl, 51br, 55br; Arteaga Collection, Lima/e.t. archive: 15cr; Biblioteca Medicea Laurenziana, Florence: 14acl, 48al, 51c; Biblioteca Nacional, Madrid/Bridgeman Art Library: 62cl; Biblioteca Nazionale Centrale, Florence: 21al/Photo - Scala: 35cl, 37al; Bibliothèque de l'Assemblée Nationale, Paris: 30bl, 56bl, 59bl; Bristol Museums and Art Gallery: 29br, 46c, 49bl, 62br;

British Library/Bridgeman Art Library: 17c, 19al; British Museum/Bridgeman Art Library: 54bl; J.L Charmet: 37bl, 44bl; Bruce Coleman Ltd: 16ar, 19ar, 60ar, 61al, 61ac; Dorig/Hutchison Library: 7ar, 30cl, 34ar; e.t. archive: 22c, 32al, 33acl, 38c, 40cr, 51br, 57c, 58al; Mary Evans Picture Library: 33cl, 45ac, 62bl/Explorer: 40al; Robert Harding Picture Library: 11bl, 17ac, 18cr, 18bl; Michael Holford: 16c, 17ar, 33bl, 54br, 56al; Hutchison Library: 59ar; Kimball Morrison, South American Pictures: 18ar; Tony Morrison, South American Pictures: 13al, 13br, 15bc, 18cl, 27al, 27acl, 30ar, 33ar, 40bc, 42al, 42ar; Museo d'America, Madrid/Photo Scala: 6br; Museum Für Vülkerkunde, Vienna: 49cr; Museum of Mankind/Bridgeman Art Library: 26acl, 52br; National Palace, Mexico City/Giraudon/ Bridgeman Art Library: (detail, Diego Rivera 'La Civilisation Zapotheque') 9bl, (detail, Diego Rivera 'Cultivation of Maize') 24bc, (detail, Diego Rivera 'The Market of Tenochtitlan') 53bl, /e.t.

archive 26c, (detail, Diego Rivera 'Tarascan Civilisation') 42cr; Peter Newark: 59cr; NHPA/Bernard: 13acl/Woodfall: 19b; Pate/Hutchison Library: 17acr; Private Collection/Bridgeman Art Library: 63br; Rietberg Museum, Zurich: 10bl; Nick Saunders/Barbara Heller: 18c, 19acl, 23al, 31ar, 63ar; Ronald Sheridan/Ancient Art and Architecture Collection: 51acr; South American Pictures: 34c; University Museum, Cuzco/e.t. archive: 10ar; Werner Forman Archive/Anthropology Museum, Veracruz: 9ar,/Edward H. Merrin Gallery, New York: 45ar,/National Museum of Anthropology, Mexico City: 53al; Michel Zabé: 30–31, 36bl, 47acl, 49c, 50al, 51ar, 52bl, 52c,/NMA, Mexico City: 29al.

Every effort has been made to trace the copyright holders. Dorling Kindersley apologizes for any unintentional omissions and would be pleased, in such cases, to add an acknowledgment in future editions.

DORLING KINDERSLEY EYEWITNESS BOOKS

1 BIRD
2 ROCKS & MINERALS
3 SKELETON
4 ARMS & ARMOR
5 TREE
6 POND & RIVER
7 BUTTERFLY & MOTH
8 SPORTS
9 SHELL
10 EARLY HUMANS
11 MAMMAL
12 MUSIC
13 DINOSAUR
14 PLANT
15 SEASHORE
16 FLAG
17 INSECT
18 MONEY
19 FOSSIL
20 FISH
21 CAR
22 FLYING MACHINE
23 ANCIENT EGYPT
24 ANCIENT ROME
25 CRYSTAL & GEM
26 REPTILE
27 INVENTION
28 WEATHER
29 CAT
30 BIBLE LANDS
31 EXPLORER
32 DOG
33 HORSE
34 FILM
35 COSTUME
36 BOAT
37 ANCIENT GREECE
38 VOLCANO & EARTHQUAKE
39 TRAIN
40 SHARK
41 AMPHIBIAN
42 ELEPHANT
43 KNIGHT
44 MUMMY
45 COWBOY
46 WHALE
47 AZTEC, INCA & MAYA
48 BOOK
49 CASTLE
50 VIKING
51 DESERT
52 PREHISTORIC LIFE
53 PYRAMID
54 JUNGLE
55 ANCIENT CHINA
56 ARCHEOLOGY
57 ARCTIC & ANTARCTIC
58 BUILDING
59 PIRATE
60 NORTH AMERICAN INDIAN
61 AFRICA
62 OCEAN
63 BATTLE
64 GORILLA, MONKEY & APE
65 MEDIEVAL LIFE
66 FARM
67 SPY
68 RELIGION
69 EAGLE & BIRDS OF PREY
70 WITCHES & MAGIC-MAKERS
71 SPACE EXPLORATION
72 SHIPWRECK